GW01607124

CONTENTS

INTRODUCTION

This book is about work and pay. In the book, we explore how this subject is evolving in an era of technology disruption and what actions individuals and organisations will need to take in order to be successful in the future.

By 2030, advances in automation and new technologies will change most work activities, and displace some groups of workers all together. This will affect some 60% of the overall workforce. As a consequence, the level of independent workers, in comparison to those who have an employment contract, is likely to double and may reach over 50% of all jobs. The speed and impact of these changes is as yet, not well recognised by most people or organisations. There is however a rising level of fear, noticeable in the media and wider society, that automation will lead to mass unemployment and a breakdown of society.

The key message from the book is one of cautious optimism. Technology may displace some workers but also create new jobs and change the nature of many work activities for the better. A greater level of autonomy and self-control that most independent workers currently experience, could in future be embraced by many more people. This is tempered however, by the potential threat of uncertainty of income, loss of benefits and social isolation.

The approach we have taken in writing the book is to spread the net widely to explore a range of economic and social topics. We bring these together to build the core themes of the book and in particular, how individuals can enjoy a good quality of life, work and well being.

The book is divided into three, colour coded, parts. The first addresses 'work and pay' and includes how organisational design is changing, the influence of different generational values and how competitive advantage is being achieved in leading economies. Part two builds on this story in terms of how technology is disrupting traditional employment models and how it is stimulating the rise of independent working. Part three focuses on quality of life and how global megatrends will impact work. Readers may prefer to seek out the areas of prime interest first. For the really impatient, Chapter 21 (towards the end of the book) provides a five-step framework to help individuals navigate through this era of change and uncertainty.

Overall, the book provides clear signposts to individuals, business leaders and policy makers about how they may manage change most effectively in a rapidly evolving work environment. We expect that our readers will be able to consider their own situation in a new light and be able to seize new opportunities as a result of this. By the end of this book, we would hope to have signalled the level of urgency and stimulated a 'call to action' to all who want to positively influence the future of work and pay.

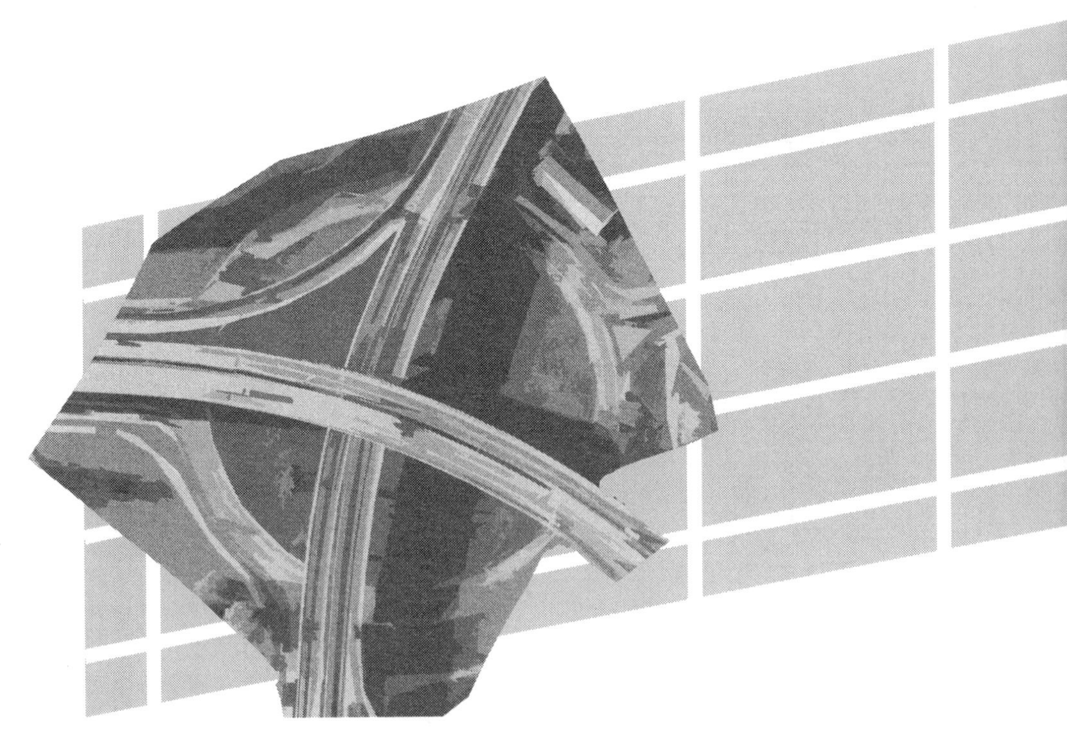

ROADMAP

1. HUNTER-GATHERERS, ONCE AGAIN?

Subject: How jobs have changed

Key Messages: Independent, task oriented-work is on the rise - This trend asks for organisational redesign and new skills for workers

2. EVOLVING ORGANISATION DESIGN

Subject: How organisations have evolved

Key Messages: Big companies can no longer afford being bureaucratic - Technology impacts all departments within an organisation

3. THE HIGH-FREQUENCY ORGANISATION

Subject: New ways of organising work & pay

Key Messages: Agility is key to stay relevant - Microsoft without Office

4. DEFINING GENERATIONS

Subject: Each generation has its own characteristics and values

Messages: Demographics greatly impact the economy - The adoption rate of technology differs between generations

5. GENERATIONAL VALUES AND BELIEFS

Subject: People's values change over time, from one generation to the next

Key Messages: In general, younger generations favour autonomy and freedom - A less hierarchical organisation and a more flexible workforce model is required

6. TENSION IS RISING

Subject: Technology poses threats and opportunities

Key Messages: There is a risk of polarisation between the generations - Businesses can adapt and bridge the divide

7. DEVELOPING COMPETITIVE ADVANTAGE

Subject: How competitive advantage is created in a market economy

Key Messages: Which countries are winning and why - There is a clear system to become competitive and it includes education

8. INCOME INEQUALITY AND RISKS FROM TECHNOLOGY DISRUPTION

Subject: Market economies have been successful, but not everyone benefits equally

Key Messages: New technologies destroy and create jobs - Income inequality opens the door to nationalism

9. POLITICAL RESPONSES TO POPULISM

Subject: Populism forces governments to shift economic policies

Key Messages: The demand for jobs challenges governments and companies - Solidarity models for funding healthcare and education are under threat

10. THE PLATFORM ECONOMY & NEW EMPLOYMENT MODELS

Subject: What defines the platform economy

Key Messages: How these platforms touch all sectors & disrupt global and local business - How digital platforms impact society

11. JOBS AT RISK AND THE ROLE OF UNIONS

Subject: Technology will replace about 20% of all jobs

Key Messages: People and new technologies work alongside - The impact of technology on union membership

12. THE SWEET SPOT BETWEEN FIX AND FLEX

Subject: Technology and an open mindset can support labour market flexibility

Key Messages: The spectrum of employment models across different countries - The need for economic policy to close the gap between workers' groups

13. BACK TO THE FUTURE

Subject: The platform economy creates opportunities for independent workers

Key Messages: The rise, fall and rise of the guilds - New technologies are creating different forms of organisation

14. THE EMERGING POWER OF ENTREPRENEURSHIP

Subject: The concept of entrepreneurship influences work & pay

Key Messages: Entrepreneurship: no return without risk - Technology is stimulating entrepreneurship across the board

15. CREATING MULTIPLE INCOME STREAMS

Subject: Diversification of income streams reduces your risk

Key Messages: There are two kinds of income streams: passive and active - Stick to the day job when you start, but add additional income streams

16. SKILLS AND ATTITUDES REQUIRED FOR A PORTFOLIO APPROACH

Subject: Why the portfolio approach is becoming increasingly attractive

Key Messages: Planning for multiple income streams - Managing multiple activities simultaneously

17. HAPPINESS VERSUS MEANINGFUL

Subject: There is a difference between 'being happy' and 'living a meaningful life'

Key Messages: Becoming independent means leaving behind the social aspects of work - Treat your well being with as much attention as your work

18. HOW MUCH IS ENOUGH?

Subject: There is a number for how much money you need

Key Messages: That number is lower than you think once you identify your costs - Learning from the Stoics

19. PEOPLE WHO LIVE THE DREAM

Subject: There are people who are doing what they want to do, i.e. living the dream

Key Messages: Taking control of your working LIFE - Enthusiasm, creativity and passion are muscles which need to be trained

20. WORK DYSTOPIA

Subject: What 'bad' could be like for workers

Key Messages: Global megatrends have the potential to massively change society - Megatrends combined with technology could make it better or worse

21. FLEX TO SUCCEED

Subject: Individuals need to take ownership of their jobs and income

Key Messages: We outline a 5-step approach for people to undertake this - Cities are the center of opportunity for professional development and social interaction

22. EPILOGUE

Subject: Bringing it all together

PART 1

WORK & PAY

01

HUNTER-GATHERERS, ONCE AGAIN?

Subject:
How jobs have changed

Key Messages

1. Independent, task oriented-work is on the rise
2. This trend asks for organisational redesign and new skills for workers

Today 23% of the global workforce is independent as opposed to employed. This book explores how these numbers are about to flip in the next decade as technology impacts jobs. We explore in the book how this will affect work and pay and how the independent worker will need to develop and manage a diverse portfolio of income streams.

When writing the book, we envisioned the following scene. It's 11.00 in the morning, there's the smell of coffee and a sunbeam falls on the kitchen table. A working mother or father and two young adults walk in and start to talk about the opportunities ahead. Somehow the topic comes to work & pay. All have recently read a book called 'Flex or Fail', and use the insights as an anchor point for a meaningful exploration of the choices ahead. Individuals at the beginning of their career and those wishing to make a change will benefit from reading this book.

This is that book. We talk about different forms of work & pay, how they can contribute to a better quality of life and how one maintains 'fitness to work' in a world driven by technology. Not only do we hope to engage with our readers, we also want to help the leaders of organisations and countries who are planning for changing labour markets and tax systems.

When we use the word 'Flex' in this book, we define it mostly as an 'open mindset'. Individuals, organisations and policymakers all need to take into account the impact of platform technologies which will reshape work and pay. This will also affect how individuals live, learn and consume goods.

In the developed world of today, 70% of the global workforce has an employment contract, a phenomenon that underpins an economic system that enables people to buy a house, get a loan for a car and marry and raise kids. The self-employment and part-time rate is roughly 23%, leaving 7% unemployed. These numbers will change in a world where technology eats jobs, contracts are monitored on the blockchain and lean companies are on the rise.

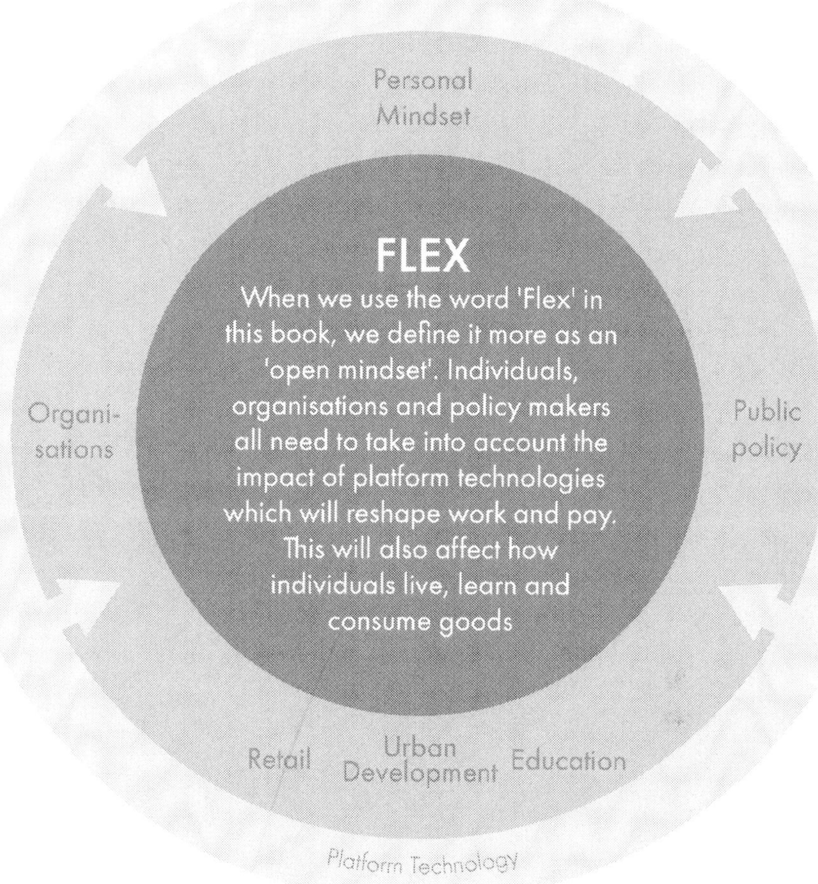

Source: Flex or Fail 2019

Lifelong jobs are almost extinct and individuals are experiencing increasing job insecurity as more work activities are becoming automated. In short, the economic fundamentals of traditional labour markets are shaking. On the one hand there is a trend for increased flexibility for labour by firms and organisations. On the other hand, individuals need some level of income stability. The new economic reality might be that people need to plan more for themselves, which requires them to learn how to diversify and manage multiple income streams, which will fundamentally underpin their resilience and confidence.

This book seeks to describe a roadmap, or blueprint, that will guide the reader from where we are today in terms of work & pay through a series of evolving disruptors that will impact all generations, over the next decades. This way the book can provide signposts to individuals and organisations about how they may manage their situation most effectively in a rapidly evolving work environment.

WERE JOBS EVER GUARANTEED?

Full time jobs that guaranteed lifetime employment were a blip in the history of work. We may have become accustomed to this form of employment by the work-related developments of the last century, but it is worth noting that for much of history this type of promise was highly unusual. We started as hunter-gatherers, then settled to work on the land, and some pursued careers as individual crafts people such as running a local blacksmith business. Were these the first independent workers?

Full-time, permanent jobs are a product of industrialisation and globalisation. From an employer's point of view this method of employment and organisation was more economical, as it reduced the transaction costs of staffing jobs per project[1] As a reward for showing up every day, the employees received a fixed salary, sometimes with benefits.

Shell, Unilever, Coca Cola and Kentucky Fried Chicken are typical examples of their time. They became successful companies, some with a history of over 100 years, and were seen as the elite of work for aspiring employees. These firms became popular with three specific groups in society: investors, governments and workers/consumers. We will review their specific interests in turn.

Investors poured in capital, expecting a superior return because of economies of scale and the continuous drive for innovation which these companies demonstrated. The process of competitiveness shapes the behaviour of these global companies: they search selectively in order to purchase cheaper raw materials and acquire the most efficient services. Subsequently, multinationals built up complex supply chains through which they sourced economically priced raw materials and often low-wage labour from the developing world while at the same time gaining benefit from less cumbersome legislation on emissions and other burdens.

Governments were enthusiastic about companies and corporate head offices because it generated tax income. Finally, the consumers who are sometimes also employees, received superior products which made life easier. All of these three parties had the same thought: this was a fair deal. As we will see in this book, not every stakeholder thinks the same way today.

THE PRESSURE ON GLOBAL COMPANIES

This model worked for the larger part of the 20th century, but then history took a turn, and global companies that once looked like a model for continuing success suddenly appeared to have lost their shine. Besides the increasing expectation from society for business to be a source of positive contributions to solving complex global issues, there was a significant financial performance concern. One look at return on equity, which is a measure of the profitability of a business in relation to the equity, during 2016 shows that multinationals' performance lags behind the performance of local companies.[2] Is the global firm in retreat?

There are exceptions to the return on equity performance quoted above. The large US Tech firms (Facebook, Apple, Amazon, Netflix and Google, referred to as FAANGs) have delivered a much better performance compared to multinationals from other industry sectors, because of their use of technology and leaner organisational design.

From an outsider's perspective, multinational companies look professional and dominant, whereas those involved in such companies are aware that these firms often can be described as politicised, bureaucratic and slow-moving. For those readers who work inside a large firm, would you recommend your daughter today to become a manager in one of these organisations? Is this different from the way your parents advised in a previous era?

A closer look at global companies reveals additional explanations for the pressure in some industry sectors. The advantages of mass production are wearing away now that consumers in developed countries start to develop an appetite for sharing services, such as car rides and city bicycles, preferring rental services over outright product ownership. Wages have risen in the developing world and global companies have become highly adept in their ability to reduce payment of local taxes.

This increasingly raises the eyebrows of the general public and legislators, who prefer to see multinationals pay tax just like anyone else. The FAANGs, mentioned earlier, have been even more controversial in the public debate around taxes, local job creation and, in certain well-known cases, data privacy invasions of users.[3]

Global companies were accused of creating new classes of privileged workers who seemed to be out of touch with the rest of society. The incomes of top executives have become a topic in newspapers and this has increased the political debate around inequality. The widespread resentment about jobs being created in lower wage countries (instead of local towns or in the countries where these businesses started), has taken center stage at recent elections in the USA.

The financial crisis of 2008 further fed the perception that multinationals, including the international banks, were living in an ivory tower. Corporate accounting scandals, antitrust violations and money-laundering incidents have made global companies a much less appealing place to work. Thomas Jefferson was onto something when he said "I hope that we shall crush in its birth the aristocracy of our monied corporations which dare already to challenge our government to a trial of strength, and bid defiance to the laws of our country."[4]

Today only 2% of the world's jobs can be found within large global companies. The finance industry for example, is shedding jobs in a technology driven restructuring round. The people leaving those jobs are not returning to the same industry since most banks have the same employment reduction policies. In view of the resistance from the general public, as well as the financial markets and legislators, global companies are being forced to rethink the fundamentals of their competitive advantage. Given that - at the time of writing this book - unemployment numbers are at low levels, there must be other companies who are recruiting these workers.

SO WHICH COMPANIES ARE WINNING?

Very often, firms with a domestic focus emerge as formidable local competitors, since digital information flows create easy opportunities for them to copy international best practices. Think of local versions of eBay whereby digital marketplace functionality is copied and aggressive marketing techniques are applied to build a number one position in one or more countries.

These companies are younger, have fewer legacy systems in place and demonstrate a different mindset about implementing technology. There is some early evidence that the number of transactions from these smaller companies is growing fast, as witnessed by statements of companies such as Paypal, which facilitates payments.

WHICH KIND OF WORKERS ARE ON THE RISE?

The question that arises is who would profit the most from these new companies, now that employment opportunities with the traditional multinationals are slowly vanishing? The lifetime employment model is clearly not on offer anymore with so many smaller companies which nimbly adjust their competency sets to new challenges. The demand for qualified, flexible and constantly learning workers seems to be on the rise.

McKinsey estimates there are 162 million people worldwide, already actively managing their independent careers. This equates to about 20 to 30 percent of the working-age population in the United States and the EU-15, a far higher number than currently used in most labour market reports. In this book we will refer to this group as independent workers.[5]

The group of 162 million workers consists of 4 subgroups which differ in their motivation why they opted to be independent and to what degree their income is primary or supplemental.

INDEPENDENT WORKERS SEGMENTED BY TYPE

	PRIMARY INCOME	SUPPLEMENTAL INCOME
PREFERRED CHOICE	*FREE AGENTS* **30% | 49 MILLION**	*CASUAL EARNERS* **40% | 64 MILLION**
OUT OF NECESSITY	*RELUCTANTS* **14% | 23 MILLION**	*FINANCIALLY STRAPPED* **16% | 26 MILLION**

Source: Manyika J., Lund S., Bughin J. et al., 'Independent work: choice, necessity and the gig-economy', McKinsey Global Institute, Oct 2016

"Free agents" receive their primary income from the clients they serve. They operate independently from a large employer and "are" their own business. They comprise of around 30% of independent workers. Sometimes they perform tasks alone, but very often they collaborate with others in informal networks.

"Casual earners" hold a job and receive a salary, but they occasionally earn money on the side to supplement their wages and comprise of around 40% of independent workers. "Reluctants," who make their primary living from independent work but would prefer traditional jobs, make up 14 percent. The "financially strapped," who do supplemental independent work out of necessity, account for 16 percent.

Some argue against the benefits of being an independent worker, stating that this type of worker is marginalised and vulnerable to being left without proper benefits protection. There are complaints that these workers receive unfair tax advantages and that they will face constant pressure on their hourly rates. As we we will see, there are other reports which show that this is not necessarily the case.

Free agents and casual earners indicate a higher satisfaction with their work lives than the two other groups. McKinsey's study suggests that these satisfaction levels hold for most countries, age ranges, incomes and levels of education. One of the reasons why the uptake of the independent workstyle has gained such traction is the availability of digital platforms and the widespread use of smartphones on fast 4G or 5G networks. Bringing together demand (customers) and supply (workers) with improved efficiency is making it possible to reach out to markets that were inaccessible previously. The same study by McKinsey reckons that 15% of independent workers already use digital platforms, a number which is likely to grow as more of these platforms are being developed for additional industry sectors.

The digital transformation which is taking place in today's society is an important enabling factor for the rise of the independent worker. There are additional forces at work that fuel the growth of the number of people who become active on the labour market without an employer. Think of the large pools of unemployed or inactive people who want to work and now find the tools and connectivity to bring their service (which could range from delivery services to domestic work) to market. At the same time, there is more demand for personal services from busy professionals who can use some assistance for tasks that they no longer have time or enthusiasm for. Company cultures are also changing, as we will review in later chapters, allowing external people to work on tasks which previously were reserved for full time employees only.

Now that we have seen how work is changing as a result of competitive cost pressures, technology and the desire to be independent, the next two chapters will investigate how today's organisations react. We will review how organisational hierarchies are flattening and why the relationships with leaders are becoming more direct including an extraordinarily candid tone of voice between managers and employees. Work might start to feel like the conversation in the kitchen, where information is shared openly, broadly, and deliberately.

02

EVOLVING ORGANISATION DESIGN

Subject:
How organisations have evolved

Key Messages
1. Big companies can no longer afford being bureaucratic
2. Technology impacts all departments within an organisation

Business is to a large degree about profit, although most companies realise there are many other outcomes from their business that are essential for their success in modern society . In this chapter we offer a crash course in organisational design that will help in understanding where companies come from and why the development of new technology requires an update to their organisational design. Although this might be familiar for some readers, it is crucial for understanding how work and pay are currently organised.

TYPES OF ORGANISATION

Let us start with a definition: a formal organisation is a group that is structured in such a way that it achieves its goals efficiently on behalf of the stakeholders. Commercial groups such as Alibaba, Tencent and Google, but also public groups such as the Tax Authority or a Pension Fund belong to this category. The primary focus of this book is on formal organisations.

Formal organisations have been around a long time and the oldest commercial members are over a 1000 years old. Examples of these type of companies includes beermakers, paper mill companies and weapon producers. These companies have changed the focus of their activities a number of times in order to adapt to new market forces with the aim to continue their existence. Long surviving companies have learned to respond to changing customer demands. Their view on the world is called modern, or open-minded; meaning they move along with the tides of change in technology or culture, instead of rowing against them. We will refer to this attitude as "the rational worldview".

WORLDVIEWS - MODERN VERSUS TRADITIONAL

Although this rational worldview might come across as an obvious choice for a company to succeed, there are many examples of organisations who opted for a different or traditional, more closed-minded, world view. This view the 'way-we-do-things-around-here' is considered fixed and defended vigorously. The social scientist Max Weber described these traditional worldviews extensively[1]

With a modern or rational worldview, everything within a company and even outside of it can be redefined or restructured, as long as it creates a more efficient way to accomplish a given task. Managers and employees in such organisations are open to changing their product design, including the way the product or service is made or delivered. This form of open mindset has brought economic success, but as companies have become more successful, they have grown bigger, and have become bureaucratic organisations.

THE RISE OF THE BUREAUCRACIES

A bureaucracy has three common characteristics:

1. its members each have specialized roles (e.g. production, sales, manager, specialist) that, when combined, form a hierarchy
2. members complete their work with technical competence, treating colleagues and customers equally while disregarding their individual and personal traits (thus displaying an impersonal yet professional working attitude);
3. it functions according to detailed rules and regulations, literally "by the book."

In today's world we tend to associate the word 'bureaucracy' with negative connotations. As Eugene McCarthy, the American politician and poet, said: 'The only thing that saves us from the bureaucracy is its inefficiency', implying that the very things that make bureaucracies effective also cause their share of problems.[2]

Weber also outlined the worst danger of bureaucracy, which he called 'alienation'. This is a state where the people within the organisation obey the rules so strictly that it becomes dehumanizing to themselves and those they serve. Following this alienation, this philosophy implies that being a good bureaucrat is not thinking for or about yourself, but solely and primarily being a good 'cog in the machine'. History has seen its share of organisational leaders and governments which behave in this negative way, following the pattern of alienation.

BUREAUCRACIES ARE SLOW TO CHANGE

Private companies and public organisations that suffer from an overly bureaucratic culture tend to be organized through a top-down hierarchy. In this concept, often visualised as a triangle, the many are ruled by the few. Organisations that require all decisions to be taken by the executives at the top of the pyramid will be slow to bring products to market, slow to respond to the needs of customers, citizens and stakeholders and slow to innovate. This becomes a problem in a time of rapid change. Technology is such a change, and it threatens bureaucracies as it allows competitors to achieve cost advantages and scale quickly.

Every organisation functions within a context or environment that includes technology, politics, legal requirements, economic trends and public opinion. The organisations which can monitor and interpret the forces that shape the economy, survive. The ability to adapt to a changing world, sometimes called agility, is a key factor for the lifespan of organisations.

Agility is a mindset. It is part of a modern worldview. If the worldview of the leaders in a bureaucratic organisation is traditional and the world is fast changing, combined with the rise of a disruptor such as new technology, a perfect storm has been created.

Understanding customers from all over the globe requires an appreciation of the idea that it takes more than one person to get it right. Agility is also about the realisation that complex challenges are better solved through multi-disciplinary teams with real decision-making authority. An agile approach includes the appreciation and engagement of independent thinkers that can function within a team. We will discuss these agile working methods in more detail in the next chapter.

HIRING

Successful modern organisations recognise that policies which worked in the past do not necessarily provide a reliable blueprint for the future. Take for example the hiring practices of the recent past, which often excluded women or people from different ethnic backgrounds.

Max Weber would have said that excluding job candidates on the basis of race or gender goes against the idea of technical competence, a view that is now increasingly accepted. It is important to understand that in the past, those people who were in charge of appointing new employees may have had a different perspective that was shaped by cultural norms at that time. Their specific cultural beliefs could lead them to genuinely believe that these groups of candidates would be less capable of doing the work, and as such, they excluded a large proportion of the available talent pool. Competition can force these people and organisations to change, bringing them more in tune with the times.

The transition from the industrial and postindustrial economy towards the information and the experience economy changes the nature of work, including the policies of bringing in new talent. Who are these new people and where will they be coming from?

Current primary and secondary education systems in most developed countries have been designed to prepare young people for work in factories or to continue in higher education. Since industry used to be based on the principles of efficiency, predictability, uniformity and control, we see similar principles in the design of the main university education systems, such as standardized tests, fixed curricula and 3 to 4 year programs.

In the present day, many new jobs are based around creating and processing information, and less around manufacturing. Tasks such as programming, design, or marketing do not necessarily respond well to today's methods. The end value that a consumer receives is no longer just the product or service, but also the experience while buying or consuming it, including the perceived relationship with the brand.

Changes in consumer preference impact what new products and services companies will design, develop and bring to market. Changing values of new generations also affect how work will be organised. In many countries, workers now enjoy greater autonomy and flexibility in when and where they work with more focus on team working and delivering outputs. In spite of different phases of economic and cultural development that individual countries go through, we observe a general trend towards more liberal values more generally, which impact the way people work.

As organisational hierarchies flatten, relationships between senior managers and their teams have become more direct and management style less dictatorial and more collaborative. Reward systems, including how people are paid, are becoming more aligned to value add and delivery of agreed outcomes, rather than fixed to job titles. As competitive pressures in terms of speed to market and differentiation increase, the emerging shapes of private companies and public organisations will need to change. This will the topic of exploration in Chapter 3.

Technology will sweep away all but the most agile and forward thinking organisations. The mindset of an organisation's leadership and the culture of the organisation (which is being shaped by the behavior of the leadership team), will be crucial to navigating organisations successfully through this period which sees rapid technological change.

03

THE HIGH-FREQUENCY ORGANISATION

Subject:
New ways of organising work & pay

Key Messages
1. Agility is key to stay relevant
2. Microsoft without Office

New technologies have opened the door for 'small & fast' companies to disrupt the 'large & slow' ones. As this becomes the reality for people, organisations and countries, we explore how they can respond to these new forces. As organisations slim down their workforce and open the doors to flexible labour, the layout of offices and the organisation of work will change. How will people who work for multiple organisations, but never truly belong to any single one, relate to the core of permanent employees and vice versa?

During interviews carried out for this book, we came across several words that represent new ways of working. Two of them that immediately stood out were the words 'agile' and 'decentralised'. To some of our readers, the word 'agile' may have become a management buzzword which certain companies use as a dogma, while other organisations just pay lip service to the concept. We think it is worth to view 'agile' and 'decentralised' together and will explain why.

'Decentralized' organisations resemble neural networks where leadership is distributed. This concept was first described in the book 'The Starfish and the Spider'[1] which categorised organisations into two categories: traditional "spiders," which have a rigid hierarchy and top-down leadership, and "starfish," which rely on the power of peer relationships. Agile and decentralised often go together, so we will use the term 'agile' throughout the rest of this chapter.

'Agile' has become a capability, and the very word brings an image to mind of employees and managers who are as flexible as ballet dancers and as strong as crossfit athletes. It is worthwhile knowing where the term 'agile' comes from. The main concept behind the term agility can be found in 'lean management', which was introduced by Toyota in the automotive industry between 1948 and 1975.[2] Another main influencer was the software industry, which launched the 'agile manifesto' in 2001.[3]

Back in the 1940's, cars suffered from low quality. Likewise, software projects in the 1990's were known to run over-time and over-budget. It therefore made perfect sense for managers to respond by forming new ways to run their business as efficiently as possible. Agile teams are such an attempt to improve business performance. The approach to agile teams functions analogous to in-house startups where intrapreneurial workers can contribute their energy.

It is important to know that we see 'agile' not just as an IT Project Management method, but potentially as a management philosophy and mindset which touches the whole of the organisation. The 'agile' organisation is superimposed on the traditional organigram, with the aim to make the business more responsive. A first important concept of agility is the implementation of small, innovative and multi-disciplinary teams focusing on customer issues. A second underlying idea is that "individuals and interactions" rank above "processes and tools". Both support quick responses to a rapidly changing environment. Words and expressions that are often associated with this movement are 'scrums', 'sprints' and 'minimal functional design'. We will address and explain each of these.

If Agile is an answer to responding faster and more flexibly, how does it work?
In order to reach agility within a company (which is as we have seen a desired feature to have) it is important to look at the structure that underlies the organisation. Most companies would name a unit of organisation a 'squad'. This is a self-steering, autonomous team of up to eight or nine people. These 'squads' work on small tasks in short cycles, achieving their immediate goal and quickly moving on to the next. Some companies have up to 200 of these teams, depending on the size of their business. This is to demonstrate that agility is not just something for small companies; it can certainly be scaled, and we will provide examples of such scaled projects later in this chapter.

Squads could be seen as the informal part of any organisation which co-exists alongside the formal organisation. The squad's mission is usually to address a specific experience that the customer might have with the company. The people in the squads still have their day-to-day jobs and the 'agile' work does not replace that. Squads are almost always multidisciplinary, meaning they combine people from various areas of expertise and backgrounds, such as marketing, product development, business intelligence, user experience and sales. This is a fruitful way of collaborating on an issue and bringing different points of view together.

For example: think of the squad behind the log-on system for your online bank account, or your mail account; it is important to have a multidisciplinary team that gives focus to this key feature in order to develop the best and safest interface across the organisation. One squad member, the Squad Leader, carries responsibility for the final product and determines the priorities within the team. However, it is important to realize that this person is not necessarily the boss.

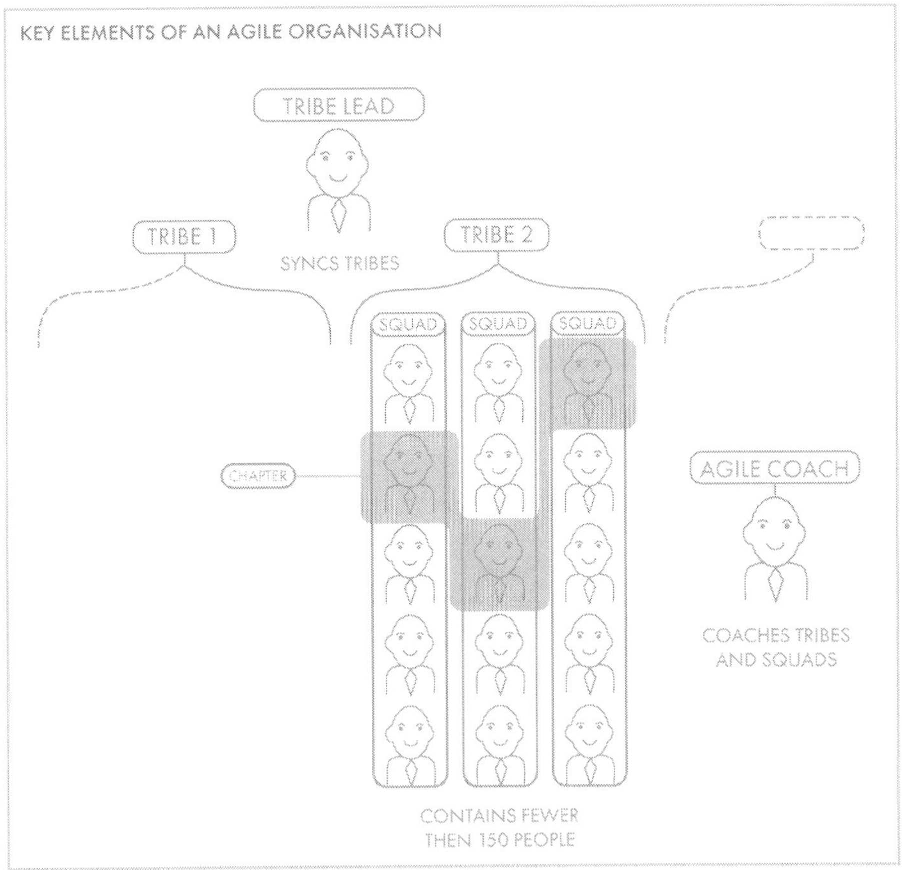

Source: Flex or Fail 2019

If squads are the vertical elements (as you can see in the graphic) of the Agile Organisation, then what are the horizontal components?[4] Collaboration between members within the same discipline, such as data analytics, takes place inside a separate structure that is called a 'chapter'. This structure of a chapter resembles 'guilds' (discussed later in the book), and determines how a task should be handled. The chapter is also crucial for the development of the individual members, and there is a so-called 'chapter lead' who represents the organisation's squad members and facilitates personal development, including coaching and performance management.

But how can coordination between squads be organised at scale? This is where the 'tribes' come into play. A tribe is a group of squads that is aiming for joint results. Tribes are recommended to have no more than a hundred and fifty people to maintain an optimal level of coordination. There is a Tribe Lead, who again is not the boss of all members, but responsible for knowledge sharing, budget allocation and priority setting. Together, these tribes form the basis of the entire informal organisational structure and provide a means to set up clear communication lines.

Worth mentioning is the additional role of the Human Resources, Learning and Personal Development people. Alongside Squads, Chapters and Tribes, a key role is that of 'coaches' who work with individuals on personal development and with squads on group dynamics. These coaches are provided by the three aforementioned functions, thereby enabling an organisation to keep all its members within the different Tribes and Squads in constant development, creating a stimulating and boosting atmosphere.

CAN AGILE WORK AT SCALE?

As described above, it seems agility can also be achieved by large companies through these substructures and classes, and it could work very effectively. Let us illustrate how agility can work at different scales without losing its power with some examples.

An example of agility at scale is the Singles' Day in China, which is celebrated on the eleventh of November. This day was originally initiated by singles as an alternative to Valentine's Day, which is held annually on February fourteenth. Whereas on Valentine's Day one would send a gift to a partner, Single's Day is about presenting another single person with a product or service.

On this day, online retail companies such as Alibaba and JD sold goods and services for an equivalent of 34 billion USD in 2017 and are expected to reach 45 billion USD in 2018. JD applied agile methodologies to handle these volumes, which were higher than the total of business done on Black Friday by all retailers in the USA combined.

Customers and recipients expect to receive their presents around Singles' Day and will order these packages online. In order to accomplish this huge task as a retail company, it is crucial to develop smooth running structures and flows of services. JD can deliver 230,000 packages from each of its mega distribution centers per day and it promises to have the majority of orders in place within 48 hours. The company's approach includes drones that deliver the packages, as this is a more economic option than sending trucks to remote villages.

Other digital innovators, such as Spotify and Netflix, are at the forefront of interacting almost instantly with their customers for optimal customer service. The new way of working calls for fast reactions to shifting client needs, more direct lines, very few meetings, room for initiative and higher levels of responsibilities for workers.

The benefits of an agile structure can easily go beyond the benefits of dealing with customers on a 24/7 basis; what about using agile structures to build planes or respond to global emergencies if your organisation is a non governmental organisation? Take for example the organisation called BRAC, founded in 1972 in Bangladesh, which today employs more than 100,000 people in 11 countries, with a total global expenditure of about $900 million to provide programs in education, gender, health care and microfinance. It has big numbers to show for in terms of impact, but more than quantities data, BRAC is also incredibly agile, creative and efficient, according to Jean-Christophe Nothias, editor-in-chief of NGO Advisor.[5]

Harvard Business Review (HBR) recently reported on companies with an agile architecture, including Saab, Sweden's defence firm.[6] They work with over one hundred agile teams, covering software, hardware and the fuselage, for building its Gripen fighter jet.

The organisations above have introduced a new language around teams and collaboration with the aim to make a 24/7, 'always on' culture possible. All of them use the agile way of working, by making use of Tribes and Squads and thus dividing tasks among subgroups, without losing the coherence needed to keep a business running smoothly and profitably.

HOW DOES THIS CHANGE PAY AND THE LEADERSHIP TEAM'S ROLE?

The leadership's team will take on a much more hands-on role now that decisions are taken by teams at the speed of light. The boss' priorities now include setting and communicating strategic priorities to the stakeholders and allocating capital to the various projects. Within some agile companies, such as ING, the members of the management board participate in squads to tackle key issues.

Getting the right people on board requires new ways of attracting and retaining people with the best skill sets. When a company has adopted an agile structure and is made up of as many as hundreds of different temporary teams, each staffed with delegates from different disciplines executing very specific tasks, one might argue that the culture becomes more open since people are faced with new colleagues more often. This supports a company in defining tasks with increasing precision for which it can now also hire and integrate independent workers with the help of online platforms driven by algorithms.

Does a data science expert really need to be employed by the company as opposed to being contracted as an independent worker? And if this person also works for other companies, would it speed up the process of knowledge sharing inside and outside the company? Would this make the company or a country as a whole more competitive, now that the talent pool is available to all?

Of course every company would love to hire the very best people from the market at an affordable rate. But now that technological developments take place so fast, and certain skills are best learned 'on-the-job', successful organisations should hire employees not just on skill, but also on attitude in terms of learning and collaboration. Since working in diverse teams lies at the very heart of being agile, the mindset behind it is one of sharing and teamwork. This also raises the question about setting certain targets and objectives. Should organisations reward workers as individuals or as teams? And who would be best positioned to deliver feedback, and is this continuous or at an annual review?

A company like Netflix has created its own language around this, with feedback and coaching coming from different places every few weeks or months. Take a look at Netflix' description of its company culture[7] followed by an example how they provide feedback, as stated on their website:

> *"What is special about Netflix, though, is how much we:*
> *1. encourage independent decision-making by employees*
> *2. share information openly, broadly, and deliberately*
> *3. are extraordinarily candid with each other*
> *4. keep only our highly effective people*
> *5. avoid rules*
>
> *Integrity for us means:*
> *You are known for candor, authenticity, transparency, and being non-political*
> *You only say things about fellow employees that you say to their face*
> *You admit mistakes freely and openly*
> *You treat people with respect independent of their status or disagreement with you"*

An agile organisation provides immediate, public recognition for a task well done because this works better than structured, year-end appraisals. Increasingly, rewards are also focused on providing the top players access to mission critical challenges, where they work with greater freedom, together with top quality talent and the best possible tools.

MICROSOFT WITHOUT OFFICE

How does the agile work environment look in practice? Is it any different from previous 'new ways of working' such as open plan offices which were first introduced in the 1980's?

Here's an example which illustrates the difference. Recently, one thousand employees of Microsoft Netherlands lived like digital nomads for three months. They were either working at the customers' site, or working at home or meeting in flexible workspaces in cities. This situation arose from an experiment that was developed while their old location at Schiphol Airport was being renovated. The choice was either to move, rebuild or to try and work without an office. The company decided to rebuild, while using the 3-month renovation period to work without an office.

The previous floor plan already consisted of mainly open workspaces, without separate offices for managers. The new layout of the floorplan was even more radical, and re-allocated the total of square metres available for the company's 'own' employees in favour of more space for external partners. In the previous office, space for employees took up five times as much floor space.

On the other hand, the public space available for customers (whether they are meeting with Microsoft workers or not) is many times larger. There is even a 'home office' within the office, furnished with art works, a large table with chairs, a kitchen block, and chairs similar to those at home.[8]

We do not envisage that all organisations will adopt an agile structure as described in this chapter. However, it is worth keeping in mind that even something as simple as a new office design can contribute to a different way of working together, which may enhance greater collaboration and effective working.

In the past three chapters we have explored the changing nature of organisations and how new innovations are stimulating structural changes which are aligned with the development of new services, products and technologies. In the next three chapters we focus on people and how changing demographics will influence work, pay and the way they want to live their lives.

04

DEFINING GENERATIONS

Subject:
Each generation has its own characteristics and values

Key Messages
1. Demographics greatly impact the economy
2. The adoption rate of technology differs between generations

WHY DEMOGRAPHICS MATTER

This chapter moves our story on from how organisational design is changing, to people and growing generational differences. Why does being part of an age cohort matter? How do people from different age cohorts differ in their views on work and pay? These are the kind of questions that relate to demographics, which is essentially the study of how populations can be segmented for analytical purposes that relate to marketing or social analysis.

Various forms of segmenting a population are used for analytical purposes, such as gender, income, geography and occupation. Age however remains the most common criteria, as it is easy to measure and comparable between populations. Additionally, age is also linked to consumers lifestyle, wants and needs, providing an opportunity to extract more information from only one form of segmentation.

Understanding demographics matters as it has a striking effect on economics in terms of labour force participation and economic growth. Since the 1940's, the values and attitudes of different demographic cohorts have been changing more rapidly than any time in previous history[1] In addition, the relative expansion and contraction in size between age cohorts is influencing both demands on the economy and the size of the workforce needed to support economic growth. This is having a profound effect on economic competitiveness and the quality of life that people can expect. Such a heady brew of intergenerational change could lead to tension and conflict, and it touches at the very heart of fairness, expectation and security within society.

CHARACTERISTICS OF DIFFERENT AGE COHORTS

'Baby Boomers' and 'Millennials' are familiar terms in everyday language that describe a particular age cohort within an overall population. Naturally, there are many other defined groups, and these can be used for a variety of reasons.

Marketeers especially are adopting these groups to develop effective promotion of products and services that are tailored specifically to values and beliefs of these different age cohorts.

Defining generational differences is a key factor for understanding labour markets too. Issues such as work participation, attitude to money, developing skills and their role in technology application are highly specific to age categories. These groupings provide a qualitative account of characteristics related to age categories that may span over 20 years for each group. Such a large age range, and overlaps between groups, may make this an 'inexact science', but it is nevertheless important in order to understand common features between age groups and changing trends between them.

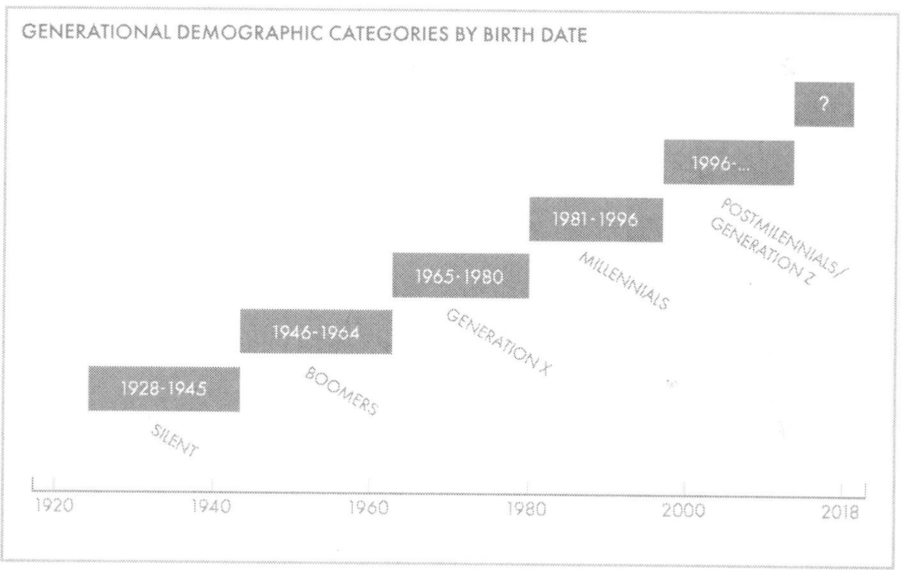

Source: Pew Research Centre

We start with the best known demographic group, the Baby Boomers, who are defined as those born between 1946 and 1964 and who would now be between 55 and 73. These were 'post war' babies who were brought up as children to believe in the 'American Dream' and were shaped by the Vietnam war and space travel. Further influenced by radicalism, the sexual revolution of the 1960's, and yuppies of the '80s, they are also the group with the highest divorce rate. They may be perceived as being materialistic, ambitious but also greedy ("greed is good" as the Baby Boomer Gordon Gekko once said).

The Boomers however have strong core values around commitment to their children, personal growth and 'wanting to make a difference'. Work is central to the identity of Baby Boomers and they are used to working long hours and value ambition. As they approach retirement, the Boomers seek flexibility to work in a more balanced way, and are adopting more flexible models that enable them to continue working at a lower intensity, so that they are able to pursue sports, leisure, travel and other self-development activities outside work.

The next cohort 'down' is Generation X, born between 1965 and 1980, and now aged between 39 and 54. These were children whose childhood was shaped by the end of the Cold War and dual income parents, while being brought up in an era of a high divorce rate. During their childhood and beyond, this generation had a greater role in 'taking care of themselves'.

Generation X is highly educated and self-reliant. They are suspicious of the values of Boomers and seek a greater 'work-life' balance. A larger proportion have pursued entrepreneurial opportunities that match their sense of independence and informality. They are confident with technology, less hierarchical and have less attachment to their employers, hence move jobs more frequently. They tend to be more cautious about money, preferring to save at a greater rate than their predecessors.

The third generation is the generation of the Millennials (also known as 'Generation Y'), who were born between 1981 and 1996, thus aged between 23 and 38 (the US Census Bureau define this group as being born between 1982 and 2000). These were the first generation brought up in a truly digital age and expanding economy. Their values were shaped by being 'protected' by their parents from perceived threats and in turn, now seek to address the 'wrongs' they see in the world.

Millennials have been familiar with digital technologies from an early age and these are embedded into their lifestyles in and outside work, around the clock 24/7. This is a family centric cohort who prioritise family over work, wanting to avoid the mistakes made by their parents. Seen as being 'narcissistic' by older generations, Millennials crave attention and appreciate feedback and guidance. They are self-confident, social and take a global perspective around key issues that they feel strongly about. In spite of being burdened with debt from college fees and high living expenses, Millennials 'earn to spend' and value positive experiences, connections with friends and 'living in the now'.

Millennials are achievement-oriented and are excited about their work, especially if they perceive this as being meaningful and creative, and as such make effective workers. Unlike predecessors however, they are less hierarchical and don't work extended hours. Instead, they have a strong desire to balance work with life, including community involvement and self-development. Flexible working, job sharing and recurrent breaks from full time work are common in this group that craves 'life experience' including travel, as part of their career trajectory.

Millennials' familiarity with technology and flexibility make them more 'output orientated' in terms of delivering work, rather than being overly concerned with the 'how and where' this happens. They thrive in a collaborative environment and engage with mentoring and training as part of their ongoing development. As the fastest growing section of the workforce in the US and other developed economies, understanding Millennials' values and work ethics are important for employers and workforce planners.

The generation following the Millennials is known as Generation Z (or post Millennials), having been born in 1996 or later. As now being aged up to 24, this is the youngest group to enter the workforce. How are Generation Z'ers different to Millennials? Starting with technology, Generation Z process information faster than their predecessors and have a shorter attention span. They spend more time on their multiple devices and live as much as in a 'virtual world' a physical one. They multi task more efficiently and switch between work and play effortlessly. They are more individual in terms of their personal identity, while global in their thinking and interaction through social media. Diversity comes naturally to this group.

Having seen the cost and time their predecessors have spent on higher education, Generation Z are increasingly entering the workforce earlier and betting that more affordable ways of studying, such as online learning, would be a more cost-effective way to gain skills and credentials.

Generation Z has a more independent view of work than Millennials. Shaped by their experience of the recession of 2008, and fuelled with their background in technology and hyper networking skills, this group is entrepreneurial, preferring a more independent way of working. They often find more organised work structures moving too slowly and too hierarchical, preferring speed, agility and more informal collaborative working environments.

HOW DEMOGRAPHICS ARE DRIVING THE ECONOMY

How does the changing nature of demographics as we have described in this chapter affect the economy? A key answer to this question is the relationship between the growth rate in gross domestic product (GDP) with the growth rate of the population and GDP per capita.

Economic growth depends on changes in numbers of people in the workforce and productivity gains, and these are related in the following way:

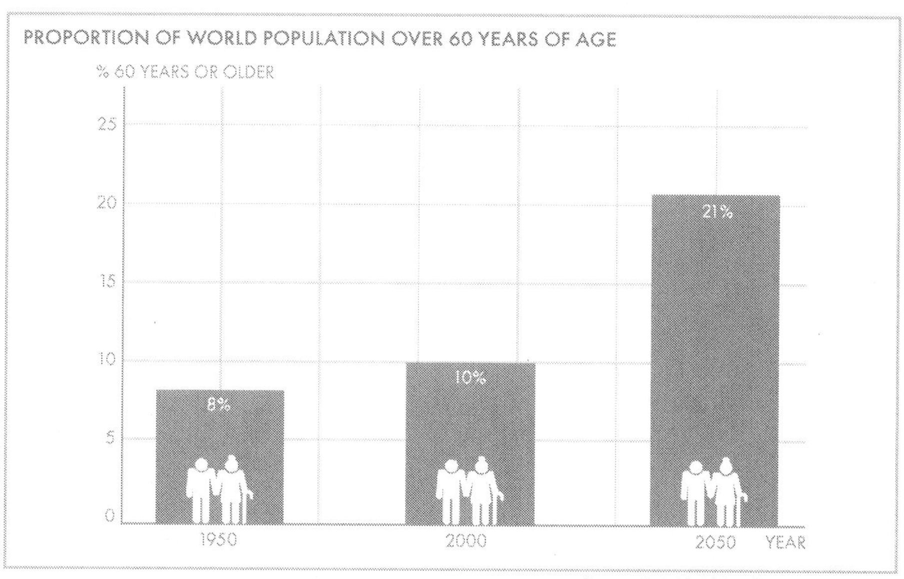

Source: UN World Population Ageing report

Growth rate of GDP = Growth rate of the population + growth rate of GDP per capita.

This fundamental relationship balances economic output to changes in technology, labour and capital stock. Globally, as Baby Boomers and their predecessor generations age and the birth rate falls, the number of new workers needed to replace them decreases, thus potentially leading to an imbalance that may affect GDP growth in future years. The average proportion of the population aged 60+ is projected to increase from 16% in 1970 to 29% in 2030, with most of the corresponding decline experienced in the 0-19 age group.[2] This is already being seen in countries such as Japan.

The dependency ratio is the ratio between people not in the labour force versus people in the labour force. It is used to measure the pressure on the productive population.

Globally, the number of working age individuals to old age individuals is forecasted to decline from 10 workers to each person over 64 in 1970 to a predicted 4 workers for each person over 64 in 2050, which makes the dependency ratio go up.

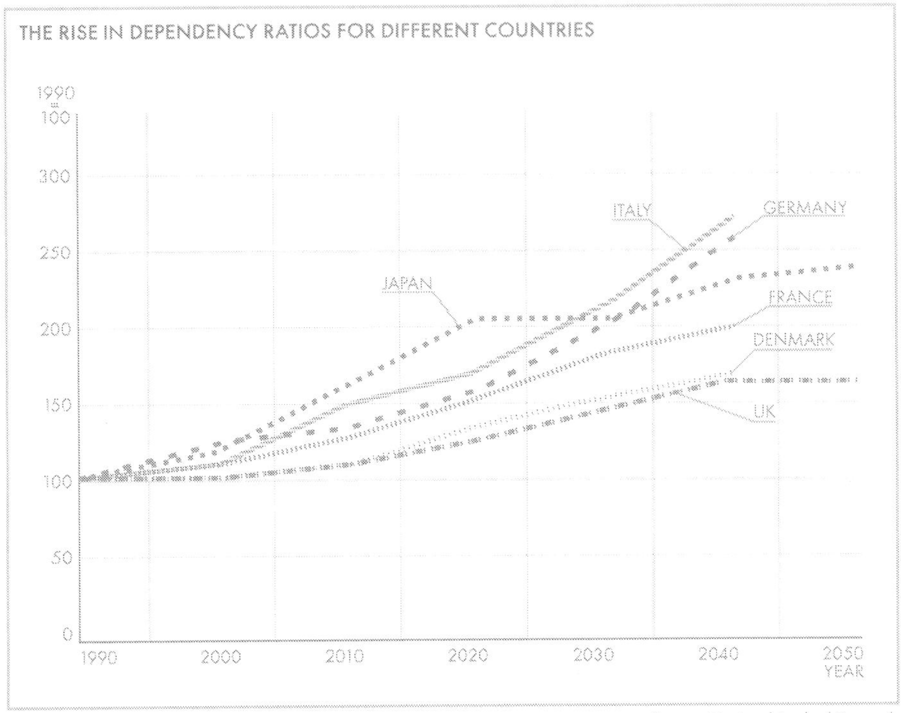

Source: National Bank of Denmark

As such, demographic changes will impact economic growth through productivity levels (for example Baby Boomers retiring and leaving the labour market), contribution to innovation (patent application levels fall as the workforce ages) and savings behaviours (older people drawing down on their savings in retirement). This is already happening and globally it can be observed that a decrease in the workforce population is contributing to a general decline in economic growth.

Compounding these forces is the rising life expectancy and cost of supporting an ageing population in terms of health and care services. With the 'atomising' of the traditional nuclear family, the burden and cost of care will increasingly fall to the state or other providers, rather than family members. In addition, the growing burden of pension costs will fall on a smaller proportion of younger workers.

As the equation above shows, either the birth rate will need to increase, and/or productivity needs to rise in order to improve economic output. As the former is less likely to become a short term solution, hopes are pinned on innovation and development of more effective technologies . In this book, we explore the world of work, pay and technology and how a better life for all may be achieved. Clearly, there is a balance to be struck between the negative impacts of technology change displacing whole categories of jobs that currently provide people with stable employment, and the need to improve productivity and economic growth through technological advances.

Later in this book we will show that, in the future, those demographic groups that have relevant skills and are prepared to work in new ways, will be most likely to succeed. Those less skilled and less likely to change working practice are at risk of unemployment. Demographics matter as overtime the labour market will change in relation to the age structure, values and needs of the workforce population. In Chapter 5 we explore in more detail the relative values and beliefs of each demographic category and describe how these may affect labour markets.

05

GENERATIONAL VALUES AND BELIEFS

Subject:
People's values change over time, from one generation to the next

Key Messages

1. In general, younger generations favour autonomy and freedom
2. A less hierarchical organisation and a more flexible workforce model is required

In chapter 4 we outlined the different demographic groups and their key characteristics. In this chapter, we explore this theme further in terms of their values and beliefs. In what way do the values of Millennials and Generation Z differ from their predecessors? What are their beliefs about work and how will this impact on organisational design? How will older workers fare as life expectancy increases and retirement benefits become less certain?

A better understanding of these factors is key to answering the question: how can we make work better in the future for individuals and organisations, while maintaining a level of economic growth needed for a sustainable society?

GENERATIONAL VALUES, BELIEFS AND THEIR IMPACT ON WORK

Overall, Millennials and Generation Z have strong values and beliefs which differ from those of the Baby Boomers and Generation X. These are influencing the way they work, who they work for and what they want to get out of work. For younger workers, their engagement from an early age with digital technologies dictates their desire for a more flexible way of working in terms of environment, hours and roles. However, we are well aware that generalisations around demographics may be dangerous, and that our description in this chapter may appear as a stereotype based mainly around people in developed economies. In other parts of the world, and across cultures, very different views may be expressed which we respect, acknowledge and celebrate.

In start-ups and more agile organisations, hierarchy, job titles and authority are rapidly giving way to a working model that is more flexible, goal oriented and collaborative. The meaning of the work itself is being questioned by younger generations who correlate this directly with their own values, especially around ethics, the environment and diversity. All of this is being underpinned by the rapid advance in technology itself and social networks that 'glue' these demographic subgroups together in an immediate and compelling way.

Both these demographic groups take a more creative approach to their work, but need constant reassurance and feedback in order to stay positive. Mentoring is important to them as they want to develop their work skills and know that lifetime learning is key to getting on.

The work environment for these younger demographic groups is crucial to their engagement and productivity. They seek a supportive social network, want more flexible work arrangements and crucially want to feel they are making a difference. They have high expectations of both what they can achieve and the working environment that they experience. Lifestyle tends to trump work advancement should this be perceived by them as a serious disruption to their core needs.

Generation Z is different still, with 72% of teens saying that they want to start their own business, a belief that has been shaped by the uncertainty of the recession of 2008 and the impact this has had on their families and upbringing.[1] Through their digital footprint, they are the first truly global generation in terms of their thinking and outlook. This generation however is prone to changing jobs more frequently and seeking new experiences.

A driving force with the emerging Millennials and Generation Z is that they are becoming more liberal. In fact, liberal values over the past 30 years have steadily increased across all generational groups. A finding that does not regress as they get older.[2] Pinker comments that this finding is both across generations and regions, and has profound sociological implications on the ways people will live and work.[3]

The emerging theme is how changing beliefs will challenge traditional working structures in terms of how fast these can change and how broad an impact this will have. The transition from a job that pays the bills, to questioning the very nature of work itself, is becoming ever more apparent. Evidence is growing that ethical values are an increasing influence for the new generation of workers. Their beliefs that certain industries are not compatible with their own ethical stance has come out strongly in the interviews we carried out. The idea of working in industries such as oil and gas, agrichemicals, online betting and armaments manufacturing jarred with some of our younger interviewees whose views on the environment, climate change and rising inequality made working in these sectors incompatible with their beliefs.

Even more fundamentally, the whole concept of capitalism and working in a 'for

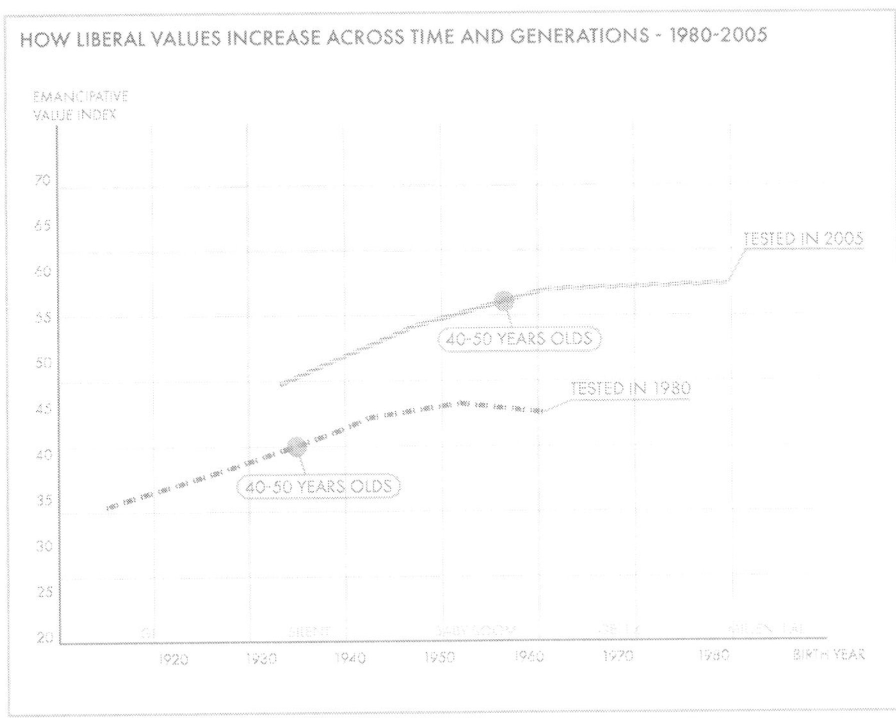

Source: Pinker S, Enlightment Now: The Case for Reason, Science, Humanism and Progress (Viking, 2016) and Welzel 2013

profit' organisation generates a strong reaction in an increasingly polarised younger demographic grouping. With its roots in the 2008 recession and economists such as Thomas Piketty challenging the nature of fairness in society, there is a rise in the number of younger workers engaged in the 'not for profit' sector, including the voluntary sector and social enterprises.[4] Those who have made the change report higher job satisfaction, improved relationships with stakeholders and closer conformity with their educational profile.[5]

DEMOGRAPHICS OF THE CHANGING WORLD OF WORK

In spite of the technological ability and creative energy emerging from a younger generation of workers, those with lower skill levels and educational achievement will in future face the risk of underemployment in a world of increasing technology disruption.

A recent report by PwC compares labour market competitiveness across countries.[6] Their analysis points to the potential long term gain of GDP for OECD countries of $1.2 trillion if the level of young people aged 20-24 'not in employment, education or training' (NEETS) were lowered to the current level of that in Germany. Germany has been able to demonstrate that an increase in the level of technical training, apprenticeships and studies that include science, technology, engineering and maths, would all contribute to this goal.

Millennial workers are also seeking to spend some time working in different countries. For those with relevant skills, the interconnected world offers a host of opportunities to work away from their home countries and to gain further life skills and experience. A mix of short term contracts and freelancing will all form part of this new mobile labour fluidity.

The demographics of the changing world of work go beyond just age cohorts. The same PwC report highlights that currently, around a third of women fall outside the labour force (including unemployed and 'not in work') in OECD countries compared to a fifth of men. Closing the gender pay gap and promoting women to higher skilled jobs would contribute to economic growth through improved labour market participation. Policies that support women stay in/return to work would have a similar effect.

Women are also increasingly switching from corporate to entrepreneurial roles, especially those who seek a greater level of autonomy following a career break and having children. Creating an economic climate that facilitates this switch will further enhance economic benefits that come from fast growing new businesses.

Our analysis of demographics has focused on the emergence of younger generations of workers and their role in the workplace of the future. However older workers, especially Baby Boomers, are currently the key demographic that are in transition as they draw to end of a career and move to retirement or in many cases, a more flexible form of working.

Their increasing loss to active labour participation affects not only their contribution to income tax, productivity and consumption, but also a loss of experience, loyalty to their employer and critical 'softer skills' that older workers have honed over years of practice.

Encouraging older workers to remain in the workforce requires a spectrum of adaptations to suit individual's needs. The emerging flexible economy is well suited to older workers who wish to work part time with an increasing variety of online platform providers able to match workers to specific jobs that fit in with their skills and availability.

For companies, keen to retain older staff, a variety of strategies are being deployed that include phased retirement and more flexible working, as key individuals want to wind down from full time roles. Other innovations include prioritising the engagement of older workers, whose level of skill, maturity and customer service can benefit their employer.

Alternative approaches from employers include the creation of new positions for older workers based on less physically taxing roles, which may include mentoring, training, expert consulting and sales, especially in markets where the customer is also in the older demographic. Adapting physical ergonomics within the work environment and supporting older staff with wellness programmes provide additional opportunities to attract and retain older staff.

Evidence from a variety of organisations across countries shows that by retaining older staff, overall staff turnover is reduced, service quality improves, profitability is increased and the general working environment enhanced.[7]

THE IMPACT OF DEMOGRAPHIC CHANGE ON ORGANISATIONAL DEVELOPMENT

Given the sheer speed and complexity of change in workforce supply and demand, how should organisations plan and act to survive in such an era of rapid technological change? The World Economic Forum highlights three key themes that capture the scope of the task ahead that include: continuous planning, rethinking HR and transforming skills and education.[8]

Planning for skills and competencies for organisations includes targeted actions needed to manage the transition to develop a workforce that is fit for the future. The risks of failing to undertake this task include mass unemployment and growing inequality in society. Planning includes a more proactive approach to developing skills and talent required within each specific industry segment. Business will need to prioritise talent and workforce development in terms of its strategic importance and provide the required resources for needs analysis and solution development.

The traditional HR function in most organisations will require re-engineering in order to deliver on future workforce needs. A greater use of analytical tools to match talent trends and skill gaps will be required to plan and align workforce strategies.

Data analytics will be crucial for forecasting and planning around specific industry and sector requirements. HR functions will also need to respond to improving talent diversity especially around equitable workforce practices and negating bias in recruitment processes.

Creating more flexible workforce models will be essential if organisations are to compete effectively in rapidly changing environment. Successful organisations will develop connections with the wider community of a more flexible, independent workforce through digital platforms and intermediaries. This will provide rapid access to specific skill sets to enable agile teams to form and execute on clearly defined tasks.

Incentivising talent will require imaginative thinking that takes into account the values and needs of specific workforce demographic groups. Personal development, autonomy and flexibility will be key requirements for attracting and retaining both younger and older workers. Organisations will need to adapt their roles to meet these needs or face an exodus of workers to competitors who are able to flex their models more effectively.

Finally, education systems will require radical change in order to redefine the needs for lifelong learning and workforce reskilling. Such a mammoth task will require cross industry and public sector collaborations in order to deliver outcomes at the scale and timeframe needed to maintain labour market competitiveness.

Organisations will also need to take a lead on formulating workforce development strategies that fit around people's jobs and lives that equip them for the future. The incentive to add value to workers through enhancing their skills and development will become the new 'battleground' for organisations in order to attract and retain an effective workforce, and thus gain competitive advantage.

06

TENSION IS RISING

Subject:
Technology poses threats and opportunities

Key Messages
1. There is a risk of polarisation between the generations
2. Businesses can adapt and bridge the divide

Conflict has always been with us. Whether it's a dispute with a neighbour, different political views within society or global wars. Since the dawn of time, conflict has been part of the human condition.

However, there is a sense for many people that the level of polarisation within society has risen to new levels in recent years. Various factors may be involved in this such as a growing level of inequality and fears around an impending environmental catastrophe. The rapid growth of social media within society, that enables instant and almost universal interaction, creates additional leverage for such fears.

How does this affect work and developing labour markets? What are the key areas of conflict and how might these evolve as the world of work itself changes; and above all, what can individuals and leaders do to overcome such conflicts?

KEY FAULT LINES ARE EMERGING

Do Millennials resent Baby Boomers? Some certainly do, the charge being that the Baby Boomer generation have failed to protect the interests of future generations, be that economic, environmental or societal[1] Conversely some Baby Boomers see younger generations as pampered, less resilient than them and self-obsessed.

Intergenerational unfairness is however strongly felt amongst the young in many communities, especially when it comes to cost of education, housing, job security and pay. In many developed economies, confidence that the state will provide a level of welfare benefits that their parents generation enjoyed, such as healthcare, higher education and pensions, is diminishing amongst younger generations. They point the finger of blame at previous generations who lived beyond their means, whose politicians have failed to control national finances, and who thus left the younger a legacy of rising national debt to pick up.

Compounding this is the cost of healthcare for an older generation with increased life expectancy and more chronic illness, which will become an increasing strain on countries' economies, since it must be paid for predominantly by a younger workforce. To illustrate, it is predicted that growth in the cost of healthcare in the US between 2013 and 2040 will add a cost of 8% to GDP.[2]

Work insecurity particularly hits the young, adversely affecting their job security and pay. The rise in demand for skills, especially in technology related roles, has relegated those unskilled people to minimum levels of pay and an increasing risk of job loss from automation. There is still much uncertainty of when and how this transformation will play out, but tension is already felt in some sections of society, that has generally fuelled more nationalist and insular reactions to often justifiable fears. For example, there is a rise in the proportion of younger people in the US who believe immigration as an increasing problem in terms of taking their jobs.[3]

A disconnect in rewards from work between those at the higher versus the lower end of the skill and education scale adds further strength to the argument that labour markets are dysfunctional. Most workers bear the brunt of this failure, and have seen no real increase in pay since the economic crisis of 2008.[4] Low skilled, often younger workers, find it difficult to save money, own a property, get health insurance or even enter into a relationship; elements that are crucial in order to maintain a stable and content working society.

Another key area of demographic tension lies in growing concerns around environmental and climate change. A British Social Attitudes Survey shows that young people's concerns around this topic are significantly higher than older demographics and that again, legacy issues will fall to them because of a failure of leadership and action of previous generations.[5] Climate change and environmental issues could affect economic growth in multiple ways including increased environmental, healthcare and social costs, and ultimately impact jobs and economic stability, all issues that we explore in more detail later.

Lastly, it is important to note the conflicts that arise between the life in the city versus life in the countryside. Old rivalries between country and city people are being eclipsed by the exponential rise in urbanisation and development of mega cities, particularly in Asia. As hubs for economic activity and new jobs, by 2030 nearly 5 billion people on the planet will live in cities as cited by a PwC report on megatrends. The worrying question that arises is how this leaves rural dwellers with slower economic growth and fewer services. Many are feeling increasingly marginalised and disconnected from a revolution that they do not feel part of. Technology can also be part of the solution to the revival of rural communities, as people can work remotely and develop new social networks, to address issues of isolation.

IMPACT ON THE CHANGING WORLD OF WORK

In the PwC report 'Workforce of the future', a picture of 2030's world of work in developed economies is shaped by an erosion of the middle classes, increased income inequality and job losses due to automation.[6] Societal unrest would be likely to rise as a result of unemployment and mass migration. However, the report states that technology advance may not be the only disruptor, as recession, monopolies, trade wars and other economic shocks may have an even greater effect on levels of employment.

Although the majority of people in developed countries enjoy their work and gain satisfaction from their jobs, this structure of work itself and the rewards from it are changing fast. This change is generating a rise in levels of anxiety and fear amongst individuals. Surveys show around a third of all workers believe that new technologies will result in large job losses and few of these jobs will be replaced by new ones.[7] Geographic regions where a single industry dominates may be at even greater risk of technology disintermediation.

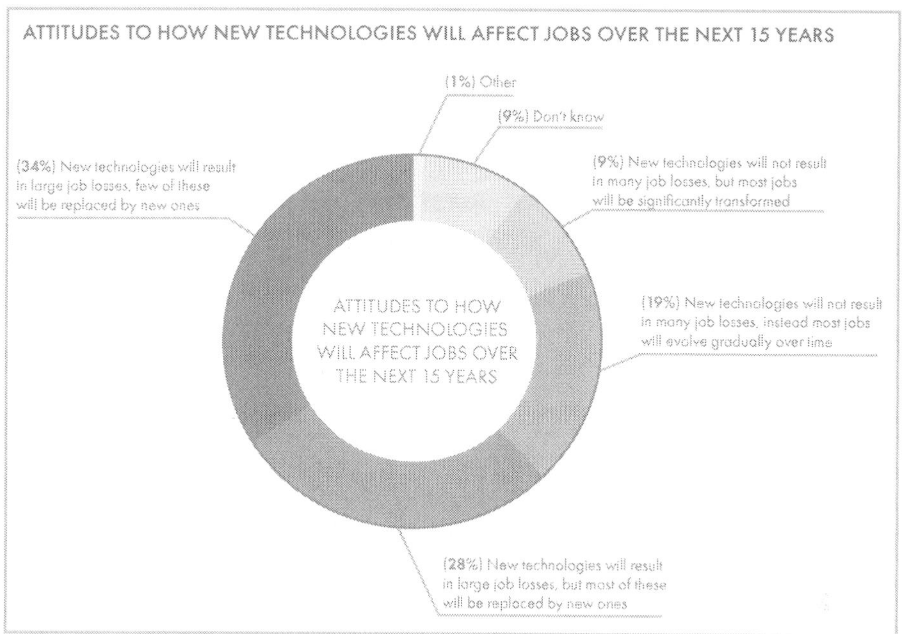

Source: RSA Populus survey of 1,114 workers (full time and part time) undertaken June 2018

Not only do new technologies potentially change the nature of jobs, but where applied in the workplace, it has the ability to monitor workforce behaviour and performance. This may cause stress and reduce autonomy, effects that again are mostly visible with the younger workers. Some 50% of workers surveyed in this regard reported to feel 'very' or 'fairly' concerned by this.[8] Application of these forms of technologies can in turn also lead to greater staff turnover and job instability.

The switch from employed to self-employed working, and the rise of the 'gig economy,'[9] is gathering speed in many developed economies, but protection for self-employed workers benefits has not developed at the same pace. Some countries such as Denmark are supporting such a change by supplementing worker's income while they look for new work and provide funding for re-skilling. Unfortunately, most governments have been slow to adapt to rapidly changing conditions. One of the reasons for this trend is the worrying fact that older workers tend to vote in political elections in higher proportions than younger ones. As such, politicians are more cautious to change policies, for example higher taxation, that would adversely affect this demographic.

Demographic tensions described above present a risk to labour markets. But it is not just the labour market that is threatened. Better educated workers are living longer while less skilled, less affluent workers leave the workforce early and have a reduced life expectancy. Such a development presents a rising level of risk for social cohesion and the threat of polarisation of the political landscape.

HOW TO ENGINEER OPTIMISM

In spite of the tensions described above, there is fortunately also reason to be optimistic. Business people who employ staff and engage independent workers know that to develop a high-performing workforce, they need to create the right working environment. That may include providing a stimulating space for people to work, paying a competitive wage, supporting workers with appropriate benefits as well as providing training and development. They are aware that key to the success of all business is to create the right culture for people to work effectively and thrive in.

Creating the right culture is underpinned by establishing clear values that the organisation and its people stand for and adhere to. Forward-looking business leaders realise the importance of developing a workforce of creative and innovative people, who are able to develop fresh ideas and adapt to the changing world around them. This is especially true for younger and more marginalised workers, and it forms the bedrock of how to overcome the key conflicts outlined in this chapter.

Earlier in this book we have outlined that belief in liberal values increases with each generation. The values and beliefs of Millennials and Generation Z suggest different priorities from their forebears that point to greater openness, inclusiveness and belief in ethical principles. Smart business leaders will develop their organisational culture to embrace these values and as a consequence, attract and retain innovative talent.

Good technology, effectively implemented, can also improve the working environment. The application of new technology is within the gift of its owners and managers who if wise, will apply these in a way which makes work more productive, effective and human, rather than intrusive and oppressive.

Improving diversity in the workplace has been shown to improve financial performance, and makes workers more mobile.[10] These forces are driving a new type of work environment, that of 'co-working'. For example WeWork, a US based commercial property start-up, is tapping into the rapidly expanding market of 'co-working' office space and currently has a presence in some 70 cities worldwide. These spaces can be hired out as a single desk or as a whole building. That in itself is not new, however its novel approach is around encouraging people to interact by providing creative spaces and services to enable innovation and collaboration to spawn and grow ideas and organisations.

Companies such as WeWork, Selina and Venn City also offer support to independent workers, by replicating services that are normally provided to employees in larger companies, such as health insurance. Furthermore, their model extends to services such as access to co-living spaces, community building activities and support to find schools for younger children. These models are likely to grow as the addressable market for independent workers expands over time.

As the market for certain segments of independent workers becomes more competitive, the greater becomes their bargaining power. This is already happening with some platform operators voluntarily offering their gig workers health insurance cover. In other cases, independent workers are developing mutual support services such as GigSuper in Australia, an innovative provider of pension services.

We still remain in an early stage of a transformation in the world of work and therefore, much remains uncertain. Conflicts abound but so do solutions. Younger people are likely to be the crucial group that will have the most influence on the direction of change. Their more flexible approach to work will increasingly shape and influence its design and it will stimulate new support services needed to accommodate a different blend of employed and independent workers.

Ultimately, the laws of supply and demand will force the market for workers to change and adapt to the needs of new generations. Those organisations whose vision and values align to these new groups will survive and grow, those left behind risk failure.

07

DEVELOPING COMPETITIVE ADVANTAGE

Subject:
How competitive advantage is created in a market economy

Key Messages
1. Which countries are winning and why
2. There is a clear approach to become competitive and it includes education

In the previous chapters we have explored some generational differences and how markets for independent workers may evolve. We now turn to the macro environment and specifically look at competitive advantage across global economies. This is important for individuals, as economics affect politics (and vice versa), which ultimately have an effect on local businesses, jobs and people.

In the next three chapters, we address factors that determine whether countries are winning, in terms of gaining competitive advantage. We examine the risks from technology disruption including inequality, and explore how this is affecting politics and society. After reading this chapter, one should have a good understanding of how competitive advantage is created. This chapter will briefly analyse the best and worst global economies. It will also examine the political and social factors of those economies before discussing how education contributes to an effective economic system.

In current times, technological advances, globalisation, and the rapid growth of the Fourth Industrial Revolution (4IR) have created unprecedented gains for many countries. However, the benefits from the global transfer of goods, services, people and ideas have not been fully realised in countries that have experienced economic, political, and cultural problems.

Schwab and Zahidi have illustrated this by stating: "This [globalisation] has in part contributed to the rise of polarized political debate and populist, nationalist and, at times, extremist agendas, both in the West and in emerging markets"[1] It is important to define competitive advantage as it relates to global market economies, in order to better understand the surrounding political, social, and economic factors of global competitiveness.

Amadeo defines a competitive advantage as follows: "A competitive advantage is what makes an entity's goods or services superior to all of a customer's other choices"[2] Although the term competitive advantage is commonly used in business, the strategies can be applied to any organisation, country, or individual in a competitive environment (n.p.). There are a number of ways to define global competitiveness, and virtually all definitions mention drivers of productivity. However, for the purpose of this chapter, we will use the definition set by the IMD World Competitiveness Center: "competitiveness is the extent to which a country is able to foster an environment in which enterprises can generate sustainable value".

WORLD COMPETITIVENESS AND FACTORS THAT UNDERPIN ECONOMIC SUCCESS

The mission of IMD World Competitiveness Center (IMD WCC) is to help countries achieve prosperity and a higher quality of life for their citizens. The rankings of the IMD World Competitiveness Center are intended to be used and interpreted to gain competitiveness. Competitiveness should be viewed as both a tool and an objective of economic policy to promote prosperity.

The IMD World Competitiveness Yearbook (WCY) has to a large extent been developed by one of the writers on our team, Professor Arturo Bris, so we are able to give in-depth insights of this report which measures the degree of competitiveness of countries since 1989. In the 2018 report, 250 indicators were used to measure competitiveness, which were grouped into four factors:

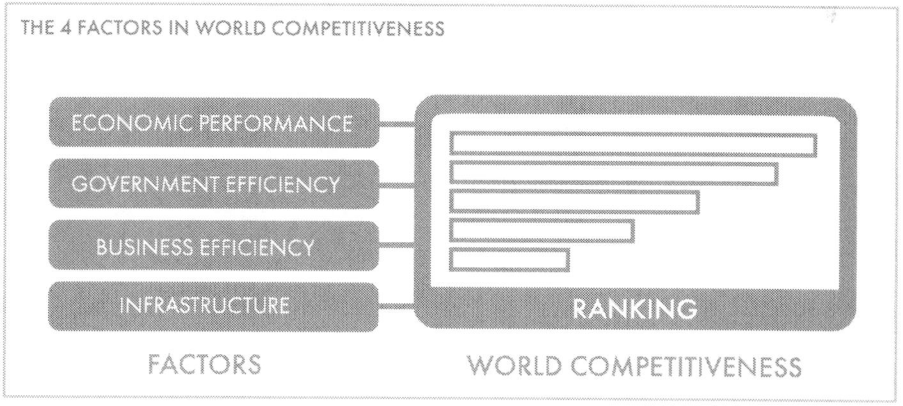

IMD World Competitiveness Center

The IMD World Competitiveness Ranking analyzes 63 economies covered by the WCY. The rankings are calculated on the basis of the 50 ranked criteria: 30 hard and 20 survey data. We provide a comprehensive summary of these rankings in Appendix A.

A summary from historic data which is provided by the WCY shows that economies that possess the best potential for offering a better quality of life appear to do well in at least two of the four main factors described above, although no two countries take the same approach. On the opposing pages, we will provide a systematic and detailed review of three top performing countries within the IMD WCC Ranking: The US, Hong-Kong and Singapore.

The US, which comes first in the recent World Competitiveness rankings, does well in the areas of infrastructure and economic performance, which can be attributed to the entrepreneurial culture and political system.

Hong-Kong, another 'top-five' winner in global competitiveness, has had a uniquely different political system and social culture, which has created an environment conducive to economic growth and competitiveness. Hong-Kong does well in government efficiency and business efficiency, but lags behind the US in other areas. Singapore, which comes third in the recent World Competitiveness rankings, has an 'economic freedom' score of 88.8, which means it is the 2nd 'freest' in the Index.

POLITICAL SYSTEMS AND THEIR RELATIONSHIP TO COMPETITIVENESS

Hong Kong

Hong Kong, which comes second in the recent World Competitiveness rankings, has one of the most unique political systems in the world which inadvertently creates the freest economic system in the world. Hong Kong is located in China but has a more competitive and prosperous economy than mainland China. According the Hong Kong Index of Economic Freedom of 2018, Hong Kong became part of the People's Republic of China (PRC) in 1997. Carrie Lam started a five-year term as chief executive in July 2017. The Index of Economic Freedom Hong Kong (2018) stated:

Under the "one country, two systems" agreement, China promised not to impose its socialist policies on Hong Kong and to allow Hong Kong a high degree of autonomy in all matters except foreign and defense policy for 50 years. This policy has been strained by PRC political interference in recent years, but Hong Kong's open and market-driven economy continues to flourish, increasingly integrated with the mainland through trade, tourism, and financial links. (p.214).[3]

Foreign trade and investment leaves Hong Kong vulnerable in many ways. It is susceptible to global financial-market volatility even more than any other economy, especially slowness that could occur in the global economy. Private Property owners are enshrined in the Basic Law. Commercial and company laws enforce contracts and protect corporate rights. Ironically, the judiciary is independent, however the city of Beijing has the power to make final constitutional interpretations, which limits the power of Hong Kong's Court of Final Appeal.

According to the Index of Economic Freedom Hong Kong (2018), the standard income tax rate is 15 percent, but the highest corporate tax rate is only 16.5 percent. The tax system is very simple and effective. The collective tax burden is about 13.9 percent of total domestic income. Government spending has amounted to 18.0 percent of total output (GDP) since 2015, and budget surpluses averages 2.9 percent of GDP. The public debt is 0.1 percent of GDP. All business work within a transparent regulatory framework.

Hong Kong made it easier for entrepreneurs by reducing the business registration fee and continues to regulate less and less. The labour laws are enforced but not hard to follow. Hong Kong has very few price controls, but the government subsidizes and regulates "residential rents and prices for telecommunications, public transport, and electricity" (p.215).

This is an example of a unique governing system that works for the people of Hong Kong, although it is very different from any other political system in the world. The subsidies provided by the government, the simple tax system is effective for citizens, but also for beneficial for businesses.

Singapore

Singapore, which comes third in the recent World Competitiveness rankings, has an 'economic freedom' score of 88.8, which means it is the 2nd 'freest' in the Index, following Hong Kong. According to the Index of Economic Freedom Singapore (2018), Singapore has implemented improvements in the integrity of government, labour freedom, and property rights. Singapore is ranked 2nd among 43 countries in the Asia–Pacific, and overall score is above the regional and world averages. Singapore like Hong Kong is uniquely different from any other economy in the world. Singapore developed free-market economy owes freedom to its open and corruption-free business environment, monetary policies, and a transparent legal system.

The government is very careful with its implementation of industrial policy which serves as a catalyst for economic development and diversification. According Index of Economic Freedom Singapore (2018):

Well-secured property rights promote entrepreneurship and productivity growth effectively. A societal intolerance of corruption strongly undergirds the rule of law. Singapore is one of the world's most prosperous nations. Despite an active parliamentary opposition, it has been ruled by one party, the People's Action Party (PAP), since independence from the U.K. in 1965. (p.368).[4]

Some civil liberties continue to be restricted, but the PAP embraces economic liberalisation and international trade. Singapore is similar to Hong Kong in the way that it is a service-oriented economy.[5] Singapore has significant manufacturing output including electronics and chemicals, but is also in a very well positioned geographic location. It operates one of the world's largest ports, exporting amongst other things, integrated circuits, refined petroleum, and computers. Property rights are protected, and contracts are enforced. Singapore has one of Asia's stronger intellectual property rights regimes, and also has been labeled as one of the world's least corrupt countries. Chen stated, "the Government of Singapore Investment Corporation (GIC) is a government-owned company assigned to manage Singapore's sovereign wealth fund".[6]

Each country takes a different path towards competitiveness linked to a country's government, culture and openness. Venezuela, which came bottom of the recent competitive rankings, suffered from political instability which harmed its competitiveness and caused it to remain stagnant. The people of Venezuela suffer because they cannot obtain a better quality of life which will ultimately lead to violence, according to Ted Gurr's Relative Deprivation Theory. This theory states that when people do what it takes to obtain a better quality of life, but never experience a shift upward on the socio-economic spectrum, they will eventually resort to violence.[7]

Another example of a dictatorship that slows economic growth would be Kim Jong-un and North Korea. North Korea is not open, transparent, or free, and the North Korean people are deprived in many ways due to the political system. Contrast this to Singapore where the government has been opening the domestic market up to foreign banks. As a consequence, currently more than 95 percent of banks in Singapore are foreign owned.

Effective governments must have an efficient tax system in place, and there has to be a comparative advantage. Often, the comparative advantage may be service or labour. The index of Economic Freedom Singapore also stated, "trade is extremely important to Singapore's economy; the combined value of exports and imports equals 318 percent of GDP. Essentially, there are no tariffs. Nontariff barriers impede some trade". The corporate tax rates for both countries are significantly low which means more foreigners have an incentive to invest. This takes us to the next example of a political system and its relationship to competitive advantage.

United States

> The United States has one of the world's richest and most diverse economies. President Trump was elected in November 2016 and his outlook was very different from his predecessor's with regard to regulatory, tax, and trade policies. The Republican Party held a slim majority in Congress, but in 2017 was still unable to fulfill promises to dismantle major legislation such as the Affordable Care Act, although it implemented major reforms to the tax code at the end of that year. President Trump ordered White House aides to draft a tax plan that reduced the corporate tax rate to 15%, even if that created

a loss of revenue during his first year in office[8] Trump was unable to get the corporate tax rate reduced to 15%, but it was a significant reduction which led to more firms coming back to the United States to conduct business. President Donald Trump has cut corporate regulations and changed trade agreements and tariffs, which improved the overall competitiveness of America's economy.

According the Index of Economic Freedom US (2018): The U.S. leads the world in computers, pharmaceuticals, and the manufacture of medical, aerospace, and military equipment. Although services account for about 80 percent of GDP, the U.S. remains the world's second-largest producer of manufactured goods and the leader in research and development[9].

Trump argued in favor of the government negotiating terms of trade, in his business approach. He also highlighted in his opinion the pitfalls of liberalism by exposing the many regulations that affected businesses, along with the high corporate tax rates, and tariffs they had to carry. Trump's view was that liberalism did not create an environment that was conducive to open trade deals, led to less regulations or a competitive economy.

Although Hong Kong, Singapore and the US have very different histories and political systems we can distill some commonalities that point to why these economies consistently appear in the top-five World Competitive rankings. These include: a system of law which is effectively enforced, an independent judiciary and a culture of openness and transparency. These countries also have generally low but effective tax systems, and low barriers to entry to new businesses, both domestic and international. Finally, they have low trade tariff barriers and a consistent approach to regulations.

EDUCATION SYSTEMS AND THEIR RELATIONSHIP TO COMPETITIVENESS

It is clear from the competitive ranking winners that their countries have developed and are investing in highly effective educational systems. For example, Singapore has transitioned from a developing nation, with low educational enrollment and completion, to becoming a leader in education system in Asia. According to Hogan, Singapore's instructional regime and institutional arrangements are backed by a range of cultural orientations that help shape the instructional regime. At the most general level, these include a broad "commitment to a nation-building narrative of meritocratic achievement and social stratification, ethnic pluralism, collective values and social cohesion, a strong, activist state and economic growth."[10]

In spite of Singapore's standard of excellence in the developed world for urban education, it still has some problems. Some criticize Singapore's education system because it centers on emphasizing role-learning and high stakes exams over a pedagogy of teaching creative thinking. Others argue that the school culture is toxic because it causes emotional and mental stress for students. The achievement gap between individuals of different races and income levels exists in Singapore but it is very narrow.[11]

Although Singapore had problems with its education system in the past, much has changed for the better in the last few years for its education system. Rates of educational attainment at all levels have risen dramatically, while students graduating at the top are the most academically competitive students in the world. These achievements starkly contrast with the relative aged population and their lack of education, clearly showing that the government has reformed education in the past few years, making it a priority.

Although two nations or cities differ, they ultimately may face the same challenges. Kent argued that "some urban cities could take lessons from the advancements in this school system, including coordinating innovation and funding at all levels of schooling, prioritising a culture change, and taking the long view" (p.4). Education has become even more important when analysing global competitiveness. One concept that can be taken away from Singapore's education system is that effective coordination efforts between primary and secondary schooling throughout higher education are necessary.

In Hong Kong, the education system has been criticized by many because it is too exam-oriented and only focuses on producing an elite, which is a similar problem that Singapore experienced. The system puts a lot of pressure on children and young people. In the news it is reported that some thirty-five students committed suicide in 2016 with the youngest being 11 years old. "Between 2010 and 2014, Hong Kong saw an average of 23 student suicides a year, according to the University of Hong Kong's Center for Suicide Research and Prevention."[12] Hong Kong's education system is very competitive, and experts compare it to a 'pressure cooker'. The government's system tests students regularly starting in third grade. Students have to compete for limited places in the country's university system. Some children associate elementary school with prison. In the classroom, students are not allowed to move, drink water, eat, go to the toilet, or talk. The teachers spent little time teaching, but instead administer mock exams on a regular basis.

According to Chan, an increase in global competitiveness has pushed the government to use market principles to organize their educational systems and utilize managerialist ideology to administer new systems.[13] In an effort to put ideas of postmodernism and the experiences of globalisation into perspective, it seems to suggest that governments should do less. There are changes afoot to transfer educational governance and control from the government's bureaucracy to more agile educational bodies. Overall this is leading to a reduced role for government as the provider of public services.

A knowledge-based economy (KBE) is characterized by the trends towards greater dependence on knowledge, information and high skill levels. There is an increasing need for ready access to all of these by the business and public sectors. Knowledge is applied through the skills of individuals. Intellectual capital is a critical asset and human resources development is one of the strategic thrusts for sustainable development.

In Singapore and Hong Kong, the key success factors include significant investment in education. Hong Kong's human capital has been a major catalyst for the city's current success, and it will continue to be a driver of Hong Kong's economic and social development. The Hong Kong Special Administrative Region Government has a goal to develop Hong Kong into an even higher value added and diversified economy.[14]

Hong Kong constantly strives to develop a good mix of talent that has broad horizons. The country needs skilled individuals, as well as more general skills such as understanding international affairs, to sustain competitiveness. Skilled labour contributes to the diversification and development of Hong Kong. In less developed countries, such as parts of Latin America, Africa, and the Middle East there is less willingness or resource, to invest in such forms of educational systems.

In this chapter, we have shown how both effective political and economic systems, as well as a high quality education system, are key success factors for 'winning countries' gaining competitive advantage. In the next chapters we go on to outline how technology is disrupting labour markets and its potential effects on inequality, politics and society.

08

INCOME INEQUALITY AND RISKS FROM TECHNOLOGY DISRUPTION

Subject:
Market economies have been successful, but not everyone benefits equally

Key Messages
1. New technologies destroy and create jobs
2. Income inequality opens the door to nationalism

Perhaps the most influential trend in recent years, arguably more than the Great Recession of 2007 and 2008, is the acceleration of the adoption of technology across all sectors. This has had remarkable impact on the productivity of individual companies and entire economies. The result has been an exponential surge in the creation of wealth among well-adjusted companies and countries.

'Well-adjusted' refers to those firms or countries that have adopted not only the latest technologies in production, but they have also established expansive capacity to continue to innovate and favorably adjust to the dynamism and volatility of the world of technology.

However, this also means that on the flip side, there are several countries across the world that have not developed this capacity. Most of these nations belong to the developing world, many of them in Africa, some parts of Asia and South America. Consequently, these nations are not sharing in the burgeoning share of the global pie. They are left behind, unable to compete, and thus trapped in a vicious cycle of poverty and significantly dependent on the major powers such as the US, the EU, and China who seem to have taken the lead on the technology front.

The most impactful influence of technology has been its alteration, transformation, or change of the nature of work. This impact has been felt in organisations across the board and is replicated. Automation is perhaps the most credited factor impacting the nature of work. In this case, organisations are increasingly replacing people with machines in a bid to enhance productivity, efficiency, and thus profitability of the firm. This has prompted panic among stakeholders, and especially workers, that eventually technology will replace human labour, and thus creating the problem of massive unemployment. However, current reports from McKinsey indicate that although technology is having a transformative impact on the nature of work, the fears of mass unemployment are significantly overstated.

This chapter will evaluate the role of automation in influencing and altering the nature of work. It will also explore the rising inequality from globalism which has led to a surge in income inequality, which then gives rise to populism/nationalism across the West (UK, EU, US) and in Venezuela. The chapter will evaluate some of the proposed solutions to inequality. These include nativist/nationalist sentiments such as anti-immigration and building a wall in the US southern border as well as movements to support minimum guaranteed incomes in countries such as Switzerland and Finland.

HOW AUTOMATION COULD LEAD TO JOB LOSSES

The concept of technological unemployment refers to the loss of work or jobs as a result of the disruption caused by technology and its integration into the structure, functioning, and strategic approaches of a company, business, or even the public sector. Such changes are characterized by the introduction of efficient and labour-saving automated machines (automation) either to aid in the productivity of the employee or to replace them completely.

In this case, the broad argument is that just like horses, which were once the prime mode of transport, were rendered obsolete by the advent of cars; the role of people in work and productivity will be equally replaced by machines. For example, the advent of mechanised looms essentially rendered artisan weavers obsolete and reduced them to poverty. A more recent example is the introduction of self-service tills, which replaced retail cashiers. The evidence shows that the technology and automation has a direct impact on the nature of work – in this case, job loss or job change are the most common and most dreaded outcomes.

These fears have been replicated by detailed studies and analyses in society. A Bruegel analysis carried out in 2014, indicated that more than 54 percent of the jobs in the European Union were at risk of computerisation and automation.

While using European data, the analysis indicated that job losses were likely to be significant in a socio-economic sense, and warned that there is a need for people and authorities to prepare for major disruption.[1]

Carl Frey and Michael Osborne, Oxford University researchers, studied 702 occupational categories. Their findings indicate that around 47 percent of the workers in the US faced a high probability of seeing their jobs automated over the next two decades.[2]

Studies carried by the Organisation for Economic Cooperation and Development (OECD) focus on the impact of technology and automation on "tasks," as opposed to "jobs." As a result, the OECD studies reveal that only 14 percent of jobs face the high risk of automation, while another 32 percent face a significant risk of automation. Their conclusion is that low-qualified workers in the job market are highly likely to be heavily affected by the adjustment costs, which are the costs associated with making any changes, as automation takes root.[3]

The risk posed on low-skill jobs is already apparent across the West. This is especially the case with the increasing disappearance of manufacturing jobs and other blue-collar jobs that have been central to driving the growth and sustenance of a middle-class life in countries such as the US and across the EU as well. However, the disappearance of manufacturing jobs from the US cannot be laid down to automation alone.

These studies indicate that automation and technologies such as machine learning and Artificial Intelligence (AI), will lead to potential job losses. Automation will continue to make more and more sense for business owners and shareholders. It will offer efficiency, reduced error rates, increased margins of profitability, and enhanced productivity. As a result, businesses that will need to be competitive in the market will have no choice but to automate.[4]

In a 2018 article appearing on the Guardian, Yvette Cooper, the labour MP who formerly worked as a secretary for work and pensions, argued that there is a need for a sociopolitical solution to prevent automation from destroying millions of jobs. She argues for a collaborative approach by politicians, business leaders, and unions to ensure that technology works for all stakeholders, and not just the businesses and leaving millions to languish in unemployment and thus poverty.[5]

Change from automation as well as algorithms also present a unique opportunity for workers to work with more freedom and flexibility. Therefore, with the right support system, a vast number of workers has the capability to leverage the positive opportunities emerging from automation and other advanced technological algorithms coming into the workplace. For example, automation can help move people from carrying out repetitive and routine work and thus free them up to focus on more rewarding roles.

At the same time, the automation of routine calculations and the assembly of data sets provides workers with the freedom to utilize their emotional intelligence and strategic skills. However, such scenarios are only possible if these workers have the support system to transition from their old jobs into higher quality ones. Typically, such changes or transitions do not happen. This has 'silo-ed' the workers into categories, job groups and occupations that can be easily decimated with the introduction of automation and other algorithms.

Overall, stakeholders across the world are concerned with the nature of work. Technological advances can open up possibilities of positive changes in the nature of labour, enhancing productivity and efficiency, and thus creating more value and more wealth. At the same time, there is a significant risk that work itself could change for the worse. Therefore, there is a need for politicians, trade unions, and businesses to work collaboratively in a manner that harnesses the positives of technology while also preserving the dignity of people in the wider society. A broad lesson can be drawn from the German government's response to the disruption of work. It worked on a paper together with civil society and business to shape the direction of policy adopted in the country responding to the reimagining of the nature of work.[6]

WHAT ARE THE PREDICTIONS REGARDING THE ROLE OF AUTOMATION AND THE NATURE OF WORK?

Richard Murnane and Frank Levy, US academics, published a 2004 book entitled "The New Division of labour." In this book, the two academics provide an analysis and some speculation regarding the tasks and jobs that will eventually be eliminated or severely affected by automation. The book's second chapter – Why People Skill Matter – Murnane and Levy argue that it is possible for self-driving trucks to operate in structured surroundings one day. However, the two academics were significantly doubtful that autonomous vehicles could ever cope with the rigors and dynamics of the streets or operating in heavy traffic.[7]

Obviously Murnane and Levy are brilliant economists, however their bold prediction about the scope and scale of technology, especially the possibility of autonomous cars, was significantly inaccurate. This underscores the fact that predicting the future regarding technology can be a thankless task. It also underscores the fact that given the volatility and dynamic nature of technology, predicting the future, in this case the impact of automation of jobs, ranges from difficult to impossible.

Partly, this is because we do not know the capacity of technology of tomorrow. We do not know what new technologies in the areas of AI, machine learning, blockchain, and the Internet of Things (IOT) will come up, and how this will influence the nature of work and the role of automation in productivity. In the case of Murnane and Levy, they did not or could not foresee the advent of machine learning and advances in AI. As a result, more and more machines are encroaching into non-routine activities in the workplace that were once regarded jobs for people.

For example, robots and automated systems at Amazon have the capacity to move pallets around busy warehouses. Additionally, soft gripping robots can pluck and bag delicate harvests of fruits on farms. In healthcare, algorithms driven by machine learning have the capacity to identify breast cancer with an 89 percent accuracy – a figure that is higher than managed by any human pathologist.[8] Faced with this reality, it is increasingly difficult to disagree with the many experts and scholars predicting tough times ahead for workers across the world.

However, the predictions of doom and gloom for the workers also face significant pushbacks, especially focusing on the current trends and patterns in the workplace. There are many things in the workplace that machines cannot do, which seem unlikely to be incorporated into the machine learning approach or the AI and robotics double act. For example, AI-run machines still struggle with open ended questions. They do not have cultural awareness or sensitivity when it comes to carrying out certain duties. Additionally, they do not have hunches, strategic vision, form opinions, and thus cannot lead. This is highlighted by the Moravec Paradox, which argues that it is comparatively easy to make computers exhibit adult level performance on intelligence tests or playing checkers, but difficult or impossible to give them the skills of a one-year-old when it comes to perception and mobility.[9]

In the Oxford study by Carl Frey and Michael Osborne the term "engineering bottlenecks" was established, which are areas which machines find the biggest challenge to master. Firstly, machines lack social intelligence, which is the ability to persuade and negotiate, be responsive to emotional cues of others, and provide or impart knowledge to others. Secondly, machines face significant difficulty in complex manipulation, which refers to the ability to handle deftly, use fine muscle control, and move or control objectives in varying settings. Thirdly, Frey and Osborne indicate that machines face significant challenges in learning and executing creativity, which is the ability to conceive new ideas and establish design and art that enhances cultural boundaries.

The multi-faceted nature of jobs, and the fact that most of them are made up of a basket of tasks, means that it might not be practical to replace entire jobs with machines. In this regard, only some of the tasks comprised in a single job can be automated. For example, the current role of a hotel receptionist includes customer services, such as meeting, greeting, and welcoming the customer, picking up or dropping keys, checking for computer system bookings, and moving heavy bags through busy walkways. Therefore, with the advent of automation, it is feasible that only a few of these tasks can be automated. Instead of the elimination of the hotel receptionist job, there will be an evolution where technology will be employed to complement the primary role of the worker. In this case, AI and robotics can provide a platform that enhances the performance and productivity of the workers.

Alongside complementing and substituting human workers, AI and robotics also provide great opportunities for the creation of work. If such a technology leads to the elimination, adaptation, or evolution of some jobs, it will also establish the platform for the creation of several other jobs. In the McKinsey report Jobs lost, jobs gained: Workforce transition in a time of automation, an argument is made that there are several gains that technology can bring into the job market. Even though it will lead to the restructuring and even the elimination of certain jobs, it will make up for this through the creation of an environment that will demand even more labour.[10]

The overall prediction is that automation will be significantly disruptive to the nature of work. The biggest impact will be the elimination of some types of jobs from the portfolio of businesses as they embrace automation, machine learning, and AI. While unemployment is likely to increase, especially among the low-skilled employee category, most of the technical aspects of work will evolve but will not be eliminated. In fact, technology will create more jobs to replace the ones lost, and thus the new economy will take shape with a prominent role for human labour.

09

POLITICAL RESPONSES TO POPULISM

Subject:
Populism forces governments to shift economic policies

Key Messages
1. The demand for jobs challenges governments and companies
2. Solidarity models for funding healthcare and education are under threat

HOW DIFFERENT COUNTRIES ARE COPING WITH THE IMPACT OF AUTOMATION ON WORK

The impact of automation on work is felt significantly more in the developed world compared to the developing world. Countries such as India have large swathes of their economies which are not yet developed. These sectors offer enormous room for economic growth and industrialisation. As a result, the traditional jobs generated through growth are still available and largely unaffected by the advanced technological revolution taking place in the developed world.

In many cases, most of the developed markets have almost saturated their economies and have little room for growth. As a result, they are significantly affected by automation. This can be seen by the massive impact of automation on the blue-collar and manufacturing jobs across the US. This is especially keenly felt in the Industrial Mid-West that was largely driven by manufacturing jobs, providing people in the region with the ability to afford a middle-class life, sending their children off to college, purchasing a home, and sustaining a decent life. In this chapter, we will look at how China and the US are responding to the disruptive impact of automation jobs.

China is not a democracy, this is significant because it underscores the ability of China to respond to crises such as unemployment in a different manner that a democracy such as the US would. A report from 2015 carried the headline "Chinese Factory replaces 90 percent of human workers with robots, production soars." This is an enormous challenge facing China, especially because it has focused heavily on becoming a technological power in the world.[1] At the same time, the competitive edge in the global market can only be met by eliminating waste, enhancing efficiency, and reducing the cost of production. Automation helps in achieving all these aspects. As a result, more and more businesses have continued to copy this model and thus getting rid of human workers in favor of machines. The response in China has largely been uncoordinated, meaning it was left up to the private sector. In any case, China sees the increasing adoption of technology as a validation of its growth. Therefore, the impact could be a surge in unemployment and a potential increase in demand for social welfare programs for the unemployed.

In the US, as already indicated, the Mid-West (also known as the 'Rustbelt') has been decimated by a combination of offshoring, globalism, and automation. The reaction has been to put efforts in re-training more and more people to fit with new working environment and the skills and qualifications this requires. For blue-collar workers, especially the ones older than 50 years, this approach is not effective. Efforts by the Trump administration to keep manufacturers based in the US has been inadequate at best. However, even keeping these companies in the US does not guarantee they will keep the jobs because they could easily switch to automation to remain competitive. Therefore, the responses in the US to the surging risk of automation and technology as whole have been uncoordinated and ineffective so far.[2]

INCOME INEQUALITY AND NATIONALISM

In her book "The Forgotten Americans: An Economic Agenda for a Divided Nation," Isabel Sawhill aptly captures some of the core dynamics facing the American economy, which have led to a surge in inequality. For purposes of this book, income inequality will be defined as "the extent to which income is distributed in an uneven manner among the population." In the US, 25 percent of American workers make less than $10 hourly. This translates to an annual income that is well below the federal poverty level. Most of the workers that earn below federal poverty level include nurses' aides, fast food workers, and cashiers.[3]

This number increased significantly in the aftermath of the 2008 Great Recession. Conversely, the wealthy people in the US seemed to have done better, while the economic hardship at the bottom intensified. According to a study carried out by economists Emmanuel Saez and Thomas Piketty, in 2012, the top 10 percent of US earners took home 50 percent of all income, which is the highest percentage in 100 years. At the same time, the top 1 percent took home 20 percent of all income. By 2015, the top 10 percent of earners in the US took home, on average, nine times as much income as the bottom 90 percent. At the same time, Americans at the top 1 percent took home, on average, 40 times more than the income of the bottom 90 percent.[4]

According to an OECD report in 2015, income inequality in Europe has hit an all-time high. The report argues that in the 1980s, the income average of the richest 10 percent was seven times higher than the bottom 10 percent. In the present day, the OECD report indicates that this figure has grown to nine and a half times more. The economic recovery experienced after the 2008 Great Recession has not reversed the long-term trend towards a surge in inequality.[5]

The increasing income inequality, exacerbated by the fact that middle class wages have stayed stagnant or declined over the last three decades, has put increasing pressure on governments to take action to protect populations, sectors or workers that have been adversely affected. The pressure on national and international politics is reaching boiling point. Hence the buzz words used in contemporary politics - populism and nationalism / nativism - to highlight these issues.

In recent years, the role of politics has grown with regards to issues of work. Policies on globalism and trade, capitalism, combined with politics dominated by corporate interests, has increasingly affected large parts of the population. The demand for the government to act, based on a populist or nationalist agenda, is a symptom of the challenges these sections of the population are facing.

POPULISM IN THE US

Populism in the US can be seen on both sides of the political divide. On the left side, populism primarily began in the aftermath of the 2008 Great Recession. The populist movement, as captured by the Occupy Wall Street (OWS) movement, sought to curb the influential power of the banks and major financial corporations in the US. The sentiment driving this movement was that the big banks and financial institutions were responsible for the Great Recession through their irresponsible behavior. Therefore, there was a need for regulation and thus curbing the freedoms of the banks to take risks that could endanger Main Street again. Other populist demands in the West include aspects such as healthcare for all, minimum wage, and government guarantee of a job, green new deal, and tuition free college. These populist demands are crucial in the US because they are seeking the government to solve some of the widespread challenges such as poor pay, lack of access to good quality healthcare, student debt, and unemployment.

On the American right-of-center politics, populism is largely captured by the election of President Trump. Part of his "Make America Great Again" (MAGA) agenda included populist issues such as ending illegal immigration from Mexico, deporting the 11 million illegal aliens in the US, renegotiating trade deals, especially the NAFTA deal with Mexico and Canada, and restructuring the relationship with China to make the US more competitive. Most of these populist sentiments that drove Trump to the presidency were fueled by rural Americans. This group has been marginalised by the disappearance of manufacturing jobs due to outsourcing or automation. Increased competition for blue collar jobs from immigrants, a decline in wages and an Opioid crisis have made things worse.

Therefore, the overall nexus of populism in the US, both the left-of-center and the right-of-center politics has been the ability of Americans to get a job, and the capacity of that job to sustain a decent life including affording a house, healthcare, and sending their children to college. As income inequality has grown in recent years, the wages at the bottom have stagnated. In an op-ed appearing on the Guardian it was argued that populism (in the US and largely across the West in countries such as France, the UK, Hungary, Poland and Italy) has been driven by the need for solutions primarily to economic hardship that the core of the middle class has faced over the last five decades.[6] In the US, this shift in politics is demonstrated by the changing attitudes towards government spending. There is increased support for welfare programs that are aimed at enhancing economic security of Americans. Furthermore, the support for the Affordable Care Act (ACA) in the US has continued to surge despite the Republicans having tried to repeal it.[7]

At the same time, the anti-immigration sentiment in the US has increasingly been espoused by the Trump administration's wish to build a wall along its southern border with Mexico. Although experts continue to doubt the potency of such a structure, as far as preventing illegal immigration and stopping the flow of drugs is concerned, it has become a symbolic issue demonstrating the populism in the US. The sentiment here is against the immigration policies that have historically been adopted in the US. Many people feel that the identity of the US is changing, that their economic challenges are a result of the immigrants in the US. These people feel that deporting immigrants will give Americans a better chance of succeeding in finding a job or bringing the manufacturing jobs back. Although the logic in this thinking does not add up, most of the populist movements often offer easy solutions to complicated problems. It shows that populism is often better at pointing at the problem as opposed to offering effective solutions.

VENEZUELA

The surge in populism in Venezuela was marked in the 1990s as Hugo Chavez made his way to power based on his charisma and a connection with the people that was sufficient to upend any form of political traditions in the country. Chavism was driven by the people's wishes for increased prosperity of the country, better use of resources, and the increased involvement of the government in solving people's day-to-day problems. The result was a large-scale nationalisation of major corporations including the oil sector, decimation of the private sector and its innovation and creativity, and the adoption of an increasingly undemocratic approach from the Chavistas. Although the populist-socialist experiment in Venezuela has failed significantly, the country provides a crucial example of the relationship between income inequality linked with other economic issues, and the surge in populism.[8]

THE VOTE FOR THE UK TO LEAVE THE EU (BREXIT)

The 2016 vote was a massive shift in the structure and thinking within Europe and a demonstration of the impact of the populist movement taking root in the UK. Demographically, the challenges facing the UK are similar to the US. Areas previously dominated by manufacturing (mainly in the north of England) are facing economic hardship. The workers are suffering from the disappearance of non-skilled and semi-skilled jobs that have helped them lead a middle class life. The government and the authorities of the EU in Brussels have not done much to help these communities to adjust to the new world.

The challenge here is that the government in the UK and the EU do not have many options when it comes to feasible programs to help these people. In the South East of England (including London), employment is predominantly in the services sector (which, until now, has not been hit as hard). The countryside voted overwhelmingly 'leave', reflecting an older and more conservative vote, whereas voters in London voted 'remain'. The referendum also highlighted the divide between baby boomers on one side and the millennials and Generation Zers on the other side, mainly voting 'leave' and 'remain' respectively.

Alongside the economic difficulties and income inequality, is the issue of immigration, which ties in closely with the economy. The influx of immigrants from Eastern Europe has been problematic for many people in the UK because they compete for blue-collar jobs. Additionally, studies indicate that immigrants exert a downward pressure on wages in the UK. This is because more and more businesses, especially the small and medium-sized (SMEs) firms prefer immigrant labour because it allows them to pay low wages, and thus reduce their cost of production. As a result, this has led to a surge in populism driven by an economic message, fueled by anti-immigration rhetoric. The Brexit vote, with the rallying cry "Take Our Country Back" has economic, sovereignty, and possibly racial connotations.

MINIMUM WAGE IN SWITZERLAND AND FINLAND

In 2014, Swiss voters, by a 76 percent majority, voted to reject the world's highest minimum wage. The argument for a minimum wage was that it would provide the people in the country with a right to live a decent life. However, opponents argued that it would lead to rising production costs and an increase in unemployment. As a result, Switzerland does not have an official minimum wage. Most of the wages in the country are determined through collective bargaining agreements that include clauses on the minimum level of compensation. The overall wage rates in the country indicate that unskilled workers are paid between 2,200 and 4,200 swiss francs monthly. The skilled workers are paid between 2,800 and 5,300 swiss francs monthly.[9] However, in Finland, the country has implemented a minimum wage depending on the industry. For example, the minimum wage in the cleaning branch is 7.3 euros per an hour while the industrial workers are paid 14 euros per hour.[10]

The move to a minimum wage is aimed at compelling businesses, that are deemed to be taking hefty profits, to cough up more payment to support the cost of living and thus allow workers to lead a decent life. This sentiment has increasingly been taken up by more and more voters across Europe and North America. This is especially the case as the service industry has expanded and the ultra-competitive environment in the global market has forced organisations to either outsource their production to low-income countries in Southeast Asia or pay equally low wages to their local workers.

The overall impact of growing populism, especially in the US and across Europe has been a severe disruption to the international norms of trade and even international relations. For example, the populist approach adopted by the US President has seen him threaten several international bodies such as the United Nations, the World Trade Organisation (WTO) and the World Bank. The US has started a de facto trade war with China, and has threatened a trade war with Canada, Mexico, and the EU. The UK's desire to exit from the EU has disrupted the core structure and way of operation of the EU. This also means that the UK is facing significant realignment and economic disruption, and therefore, has to figure out a deal to exit the EU and how to coexist with the EU in terms of trade.

The EU incumbent governments in Germany, Spain, Italy, and France are facing burgeoning populism movements. Populism threatens to disrupt the world order as we know it, and causes shifts in economic policies. However, populism's ability to come up with cogent and potent solutions to the challenges - such as income inequality and unemployment as a result of automation and advanced technologies such as AI, IoT, and machine learning - has not been demonstrated.

However, one thing is for sure, whether through populism, nationalism, nativism, or liberal capitalism, there is a need to provide tangible solutions to the issues of income inequality and the disruption of work brought about by automation. As we highlight in this book, the responsibility lies also, and maybe increasingly, with individuals. Most workers will need to analyse the risks associated with their profession, and plan the necessary steps to stay relevant from a skills perspective, which includes life long learning.

PART 2

TECHNOLOGY DISRUPTION

10

THE PLATFORM ECONOMY & NEW EMPLOYMENT MODELS

Subject:
What defines the platform economy

Key Message
1. How these platforms touch all sectors & disrupt global and local business
2. How digital platforms impact society

We define the term 'platform economy' as any economic and social activity that is facilitated by online platforms that include transaction and matchmaking services. This chapter describes the platform economy and how it is becoming embedded in current society, thereby also explaining the benefits and pitfalls of this new form of ecosystem. We will take a look at three industry sectors which are part of the platform economy, and which are influenced by various technologies.

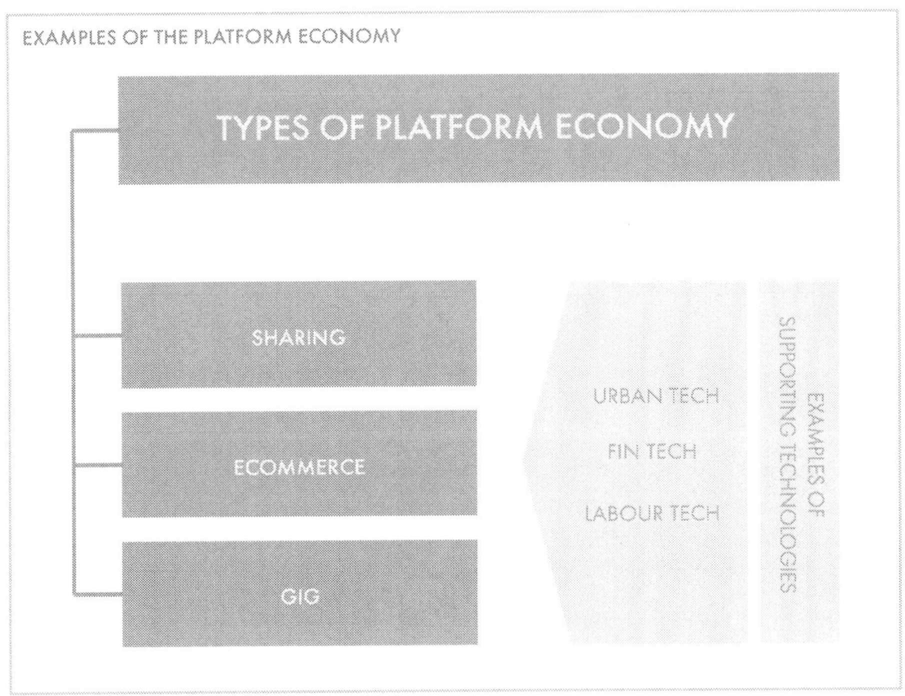

Source: Flex or Fall 2019

A consequence of the platform economy is that companies form their own ecosystem or become part of the ecosystems of others. As an example we take the banking industry which has many clients with bank accounts. The clients interact with their bank through an app on the phone which gives them access to their bank account, but these clients could also feel the need to buy an insurance or, if they are into modern technology, access a smart contract on the blockchain. This could lead the bank to open up its app to third party suppliers in return for a commission. At the same time, the banking services could be needed in the apps of other companies including those of competitors.

One type of platform economy is the sharing economy which can be defined as an economic system in which assets or services are shared between individuals, either for a fee or for free, typically by means of the internet and online platforms. It is based around the idea that one does not necessarily need to own everything one uses; it is often enough to simply have access to these products and services when needed. Unlike their older counterparts, younger generations are generally less focussed on owning certain assets, like cars and would rather rent these as required.

Digital platforms are the tools that make this concept scalable. These platforms are basically websites or apps that match buyers with sellers of products and services. The core idea is to use the spare capacity, of assets and/or time, more efficiently. These platforms act as the connection between buyer and seller, while at the same time providing trust (ensuring that people will get paid) and verification (ensuring what you believe you are getting will actually happen). If well executed, such platforms are obviously a great means to secure fast and safe transactions, which is why the emergence is rapidly growing; PwC estimates that the size of the global sharing economy will grow to $335bn by 2025.[1]

Currently, there are now hundreds, if not thousands, of such platforms; an indicator that shows its success. We will illustrate some examples across major industry sectors in more depth to highlight some of the key similarities and reasons behind their success.

EXAMPLES OF PLATFORMS IN THE SHARING ECONOMY

We will take a look at various sectors that have been impacted by the platforms of the sharing economy. In the travel and lodging industry AirBnB is the leading platform player. Its customers can book rooms, apartments or houses, and the service sometimes includes advice on local leisure experiences. AirBnB does not own the houses, but instead acts as a broker and receives commissions from the reservations. The company was founded in 2008 and its initial public offering (IPO) is expected in 2019.

As such, AirBnB serves as a model for the success of the sharing economy; it literally facilitates the exchange of living spaces without having anything to do with ownership. People who have a spare room or a vacant house can connect with a global public through AirBnB and create an new income stream. However, resistance against AirBnB is increasing, mainly voiced by hotel owners who cite unfair competition and residents living in city centres who fear uncontrolled tourism will make the town centers less pleasant to live in and prone to real-estate speculation. AirBnB has a number of competitors in its key markets including Homeway, Tripadvisor and Onefinestay.

CouchSurfing is another platform that focuses on 'not-for-profit' lodging by offering a place to 'crash for free' in a member's house to those reluctant to spend any money. This often includes some form of social interaction with the host and local community. The platform presents itself as being part of the 'gift-economy', since hosts are not allowed to charge for lodging. Guests sometimes make small contributions in kind to thank their new friends for such generosity, but this is by no means expected when joining the Couchsurfing community.

In the transportation sector, platform players such as BlaBlaCar (ride sharing) and SnappCar (car sharing) are successful and a threat to established companies such as rental companies and car manufacturers. After all, why would customers waste time queueing to complete the paperwork for their rental car, when they can get access to a private car via an app?

As was the case with Couchsurfing versus AirBnB, we can see the same form of slightly alternative initiatives in the transportation sector. Companies like ZipCar, FlightCar or Car2Go created an innovative twist: they let people park at the airport while renting out their vehicles to other approved travelling members. Every rental is insured and every renter is pre-screened. Members get free parking, a car wash, and a payout if their car is selected. Who would not want to make money while flying, and on top of that find your car freshly cleaned upon return?

Within the tools and appliances sector, companies like Peerby enable people to generate extra income from owning tools, such as drilling machines and fruit juicers. Peerby is an online sharing community that facilitates the sharing and borrowing of items from people in the neighbourhood. Peerby is headquartered in Amsterdam and its main competitors are Nextdoor, GTCR and Streetlife.

EXAMPLES OF PLATFORMS IN THE GIG ECONOMY

The logic of the digital platforms used in the sharing economy can also facilitate the exchange of short-term tasks, or 'gigs' as they are sometimes called. The gig-economy is not the same as the sharing economy. We define the gig economy as a labour market where short term tasks are posted and fulfilled. The gig economy uses platforms to connect potential workers with clients who are looking to get a specific job or task done. Uber, Deliveroo, Handy, 360Experts and Upwork are representative examples of the gig economy, and they all started around 2010.

In the transportation sector, Uber is the most well known brand. Uber is a peer-to-peer transportation network company. People with a car or bike and some spare time can qualify to become a Uber driver and earn money. From its San Francisco base, Uber operates in 785 metropolitan areas worldwide through its popular app. It's name has even become an official noun, "Uberisation", that describes the transformation of complete industries as a result of technology.

There are several other initiatives around the world that mimic Uber in the hope of achieving a similar success rate; Ola from India, Lyft from the US, Grab from Singapore, GoJek from Indonesia and Didi Chuxing from China are key competitors.

Naturally, one can expect similar developing initiatives within the professional services sector. TaskRabbit is an online marketplace that matches labour with demand from households in a local area. The everyday tasks include cleaning, moving, delivery and handyman work. TaskRabbit was founded in 2008 and has tens of thousands of background-checked "Taskers" who are available to assist time-constrained households by taking up some of the chores. Task Rabbit's current owner is IKEA, which provides its customers with people who can put together furniture. Task Rabbit's main competitors are Handy, TalkLocal and Pro.com.

Expert360, headquartered in Sydney, Australia is a company that offers similar services, but focuses on delivering professional services specifically to businesses. Expert360 matches independent business consultants, such as data scientists, researchers or agile team facilitators with clients (companies, organisations). The projects or tasks can either be of a short term nature, or can provide long term work, and hourly or daily rates are market conform. Upwork and Toptal are competitors in this marketspace.

EXAMPLES OF PLATFORMS IN E-COMMERCE

In the world of retail, Amazon, Alibaba and eBay are the dominant players. Amazon is the largest Internet retailer in the world as measured by revenue and market capitalisation, and second largest after Alibaba Group in terms of total sales. In 2015, Amazon surpassed Walmart as the most valuable retailer in the United States by market capitalisation. In 2019 the market cap surpassed the 1 trillion USD mark for the first time.

These retail sites allow individuals and businesses to sell goods and services through its platform. Simply put, they are like a supermarket-of-the-world and basically sell everything. The idea that you can create your own boutique sales-counter inside a large digital mall is appealing to many smaller producers and crafts people, who are now enabled to sell their niche products into a global market. In return, the platform owners ask for a commission, but support the trades with verification, payments and logistical services.

Etsy is an e-commerce website focused on handmade or vintage items and supplies, as well as unique factory-manufactured items. These items cover a wide range, including art, photography, clothing, jewelry, food, bath and beauty products, quilts, knick-knacks, and toys. It is an example of an online platform for people who want to create an income stream through their craft skills. Estimations show that Etsy has 37 million buyers and 2 million sellers.[2] Etsy had just 841 employees in 2017 and was able to list 50 million items on its website.

Apart from all these services and products that are offered through such platforms, there is also a need for payment services, as many businesses and independent workers depend on getting money for the products, services, gigs and tasks from their various clients. Online payment service providers such as Paypal (USA), Adyen (The Netherlands), WeChat Pay and Alipay (both from China) facilitate the handling of billions of transactions annually. Their services enable individuals to do business in a professional way without the need for an entire finance department. This 'fintech' service industry develops special plug-ins, which act as tools that allow website owners to add additional payment functionality in return for a small commission per transaction.

IMPACT ON SOCIETY

Gallup found that 60% of Millennials say they are open to a different job opportunity, and further reported that approximately 50% of the American employees aspired to leave the job that they were doing.[3] Unemployment in the US stands at 3.9%, very similar to the situation in The Netherlands. When the economy is doing well, employees and independent workers have more confidence to change jobs, as they will be more certain of finding new work within a reasonable timescale. As the economy goes through the cycles of growth and decline, one would expect to see these waves reflected in the changes of the number of people willing to leave their current position.

There are signs that certain sectors have a more fundamental problem, apart from the cyclical effect of the economy. The hospitality sector, for example, is often staffed by low-paid, young people who perform tasks like waitering, bartending or cleaning dishes as a side business.[4] Traditional employers or staffing agencies in this sector have a problem to find and retain their staff, and platform players which broker the demand for these workers are stepping in with slightly improved pay packages and improved work schedule management.

Are the above independent workers vulnerable to hourly rate pressure? What will be the mechanism to avoid a race to the bottom where only the lowest bidder wins, and everyone ends up being marginalised? People notice the increase of tasks, but fear reduced rates. The response from governments and tax offices centers around standardised minimum wages and mandatory insurance for independent workers. Increasingly, this debate has moved from an economic to a political debate.

To illustrate this with an example we look at New York. In December 2018 the city passed USA's first minimum pay rate for drivers who work for companies like Uber and Lyft.[5] It took a two-year legal battle to make sure drivers got a minimum wage for their platform-based work. Starting in January 2019, companies will start paying drivers around $17.22 per hour (after expenses) – about $5 more per hour than the current average of $11.90 per hour, according to the Independent Drivers Guild who represents about 70,000 Uber, Lyft, Juno, and Via drivers in the city. The new pay rate is calculated per ride, but the guild expects it to give full-time drivers an extra $9,600 a year. Uber and Lyft drivers are considered independent contractors and not employees. The new rules essentially get around loopholes and ensure that drivers are earning at least the minimum wage, with a few dollars extra to cover payroll taxes and some paid time off.

This change is the most visible first attempt to regulate the platform economy since 'big tech' upended urban transportation in 2011. New York City may pave the way for other cities and countries to provide oversight of the platform economy.

Jeremy Corbyn, the leader of Britain's Labour Party, has stated that using contractors via platforms, instead of employing people, is an "exploitative form of capitalism". Australia is one of the leading countries when it comes to embracing the gig economy, but a recent parliamentary report stated that "the gig economy is normalising labour conditions which took generations of political struggle to stamp out in this country."[6]

The rise of platforms is welcomed with both support and criticism. Those in favour argue improved productivity, reduced costs, reduced inefficiencies in existing markets, new market creation and especially helpful for less developed countries. Workers themselves often state they favour working through platforms because it brings work that they would not be able to find otherwise, with the flexibility to fit it in with other duties and as such earning additional money when it is needed.

Those against platforms argue that it will only increase unemployment and replace traditional jobs with ones that offer less protection for the workers. As a result, tax revenues could decline which would have a damaging effect on communities. In the early days of platform development, regulators resisted intervention, but recently, some jurisdictions are taking a more interventionist approach to combat such negative consequences, without losing the benefits that the new system has to offer. New York, for example, has become the first major US city to approve a cap on ride-hail car licences to reduce the number of taxis on the road.[7]

Politicians, unions and employment agencies have been especially vocal about the dangers of the platform economy. Reducing income security for vulnerable groups and increasing inequality are risks which need to be mitigated. These points of view and how they matter for the future of work will be discussed in later chapters.

11

JOBS AT RISK AND THE ROLE OF UNIONS

Subject:
Technology will replace about 20% of all jobs

Key Message
1. People and new technologies work alongside
2. The impact of technology on union membership

Considering all the different types of jobs that currently exist, what are the proportion of activities that could be replaced by technology one way or another? Do you think it is an alarming number, or that people tend to exaggerate when they claim that many jobs will vanish?

A research report by McKinsey of more than 2,000 work activities across 800 occupations shines some light on the question, as it is one of the few studies that looks at the impact at such a large sample size.[1] They concluded that well over half of people's jobs today, have some form of activity in them which could be replaced by technology by 2055. To what extent such a job could be replaced varies, but the estimate is around one third. Emerging technologies such as artificial intelligence, robotisation, Blockchain, augmented reality and machine learning are increasingly finding their way into the workplace. PwC estimates that seven million jobs in the UK will be lost due to automation by 2040.[2] Others, like the Bank of England, estimate this will happen 5 years earlier and with double the number of jobs lost.[3]

ARE JOBS BEING REPLACED AT SCALE?

Can employers make more profit through automation and will the hassle around personnel management be less? If so, why is the job loss not that substantial yet? We have enough advanced technology that could have replaced workers in large numbers over the past years. However, if you take a look at the job market statistics of today, you can observe that the rate of unemployment in developed countries is at its lowest level in 40 years. The concerns of employers in these OECD countries center around staffing jobs with qualified workers (the so called war-for-talent) and retaining those workers once they are part of the company. A first explanation seems to be that some industry sectors have been affected but others, less prone to automation, not yet. A second explanation is that people can be 'under utilised', e.g. employed or self-employed workers who are not doing as many hours as they would like to do or people doing jobs that they are overqualified for. A third reason is that unemployment numbers between countries are hard to compare, since the definitions used are not the same. Some countries move people into early-retirement, or 'unfit for work' groups which lowers the reported unemployment numbers.

Another way to look at the matter would be to say that today's jobs will be enhanced by using advanced technology in combination with human input, rather than saying that jobs will simply be replaced over time. In the future, people are more likely to work alongside an array of smart technologies.

Adair Turner, Chairman of the Institute for New Economic Thinking, suggests that the current situation is evolving towards one where there are two types of jobs: 'hi-tech' ones that involve creating, maintaining and interpreting machines; and 'hi-touch' ones that focus on social interactions, such as caring for the elderly and sick.[4]

This is not to say that the 'hi-touch' ones will not have to deal with technology at all, as they too will need to interact with new technologies. Both 'high-tech' and 'hi-touch' workers will need support in terms of education and training programs in order to reskill for the evolving work environment.

Technology does not force itself upon us; organisations and people have the choice whether to work with technology, and in what way. An individual could decide that a new smartphone is not really a necessary item, based on the argument that "a phone is for calling only". However, not owning a smartphone in this day and age is a big decision. It restricts one from connecting to the cloud and prevents access to a plethora of services which are increasingly essential to function in the modern world. The phenomenon that we call the 'digital divide' starts here: not having access to new technology and networks increases the risk of inequality, because critical information and services are not available to people at the right time. This gap is leading to an increasing risk of digital and economic inequality amongst individuals, and potentially organisations who do not adapt quickly enough.

Businesses are not completely free to do as they please. They have to respond to competitors who are investing in new technologies in order to stay competitive. In addition, they need to constantly strive to develop low cost structures, while at the same time working with governments and trade unions who seek to protect the interests of workers and society as a whole.

TECHNOLOGY AND TRADE UNIONS

The primary goal of trade unions is to unite groups of workers and negotiate with employers on their behalf to create collective agreements around pay and benefits. The rise of the unions was originally driven by industrialisation around 1850.

One could argue that industrialisation was the result of new technology, being the new steam machines and electricity. The fact that these expensive machines were brought together in a central location, or a factory, was the driving factor behind urbanisation; everybody wanted to move to where new work was available. As a consequence of similar groups of workers living and working closely together, it became easier to communicate, organise and negotiate on behalf of large groups.

This is where the unions started to develop a position of power. New machines and skilled workers created products that consumers wanted and drove profit, so any shutdown in the factory led to pressure on employers to settle labour disputes quickly. Similarly, employers wanted to deal with unions because it was more efficient to negotiate with a small group of union representatives, instead of having to deal with many individual workers. The union's power to positively influence conditions for its members depended to a large degree on centralisation of labour and the amount of capital tied up in equipment.

Before 1850 there were almost no unions and their importance gradually grew over time: it took 60 years in the USA to get 10% of the workforce organised in a union. In most OECD countries, which is a group of 34 developed nations, union membership peaked at 40-50% of the workforce in the second half of the last century.[5] Ever since, unions have lost members, meaning that today, merely 18% of workers are being represented by a union.

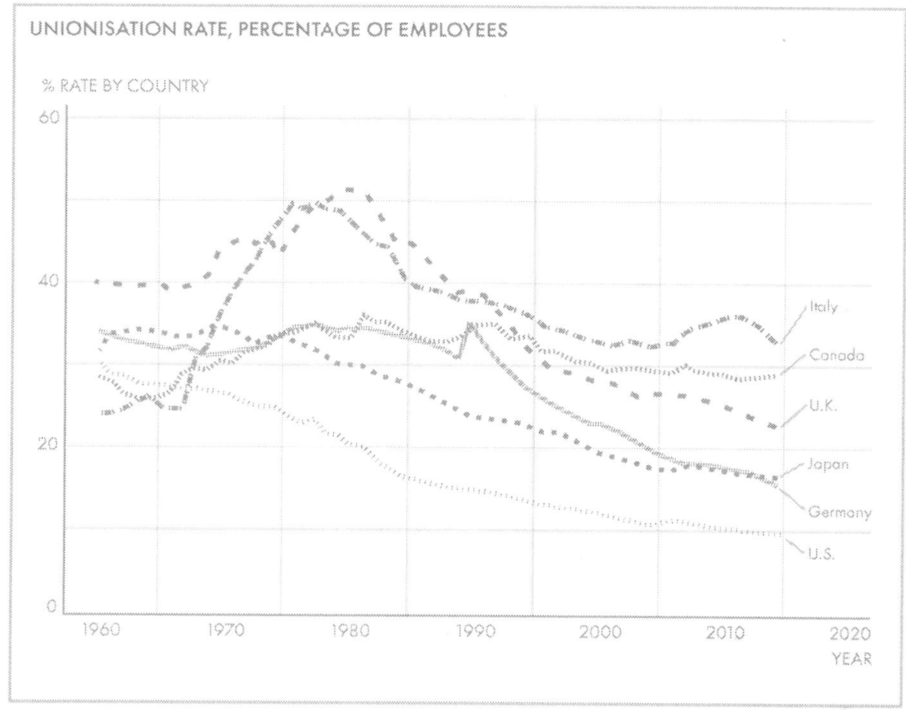

Source: OECD

WHAT CAUSES THE DECLINE OF UNION POWER?

Governments have not always been a friend to the unions, as the world was able to witness with the strikes in the UK under Margaret Thatcher in the 1980s, and Ronald Reagan in the US. The decline of the unions can partly be explained by the fact that democratically elected governments gain votes by introducing laws which guarantee workers minimum wage, health care and pension benefits. If the government is taking care of workers directly, they are indirectly taking over the job of the union, and as such, the influence of a union becomes smaller. Other reasons as to why union membership has declined include the improvements in social benefits and the move away from heavy industry, traditional manufacturing and mining, which are capital intensive and require organised labour. Previously, such industries employed large numbers of workers, whereas more recently the services sector has been the main driver for job growth. Services increasingly rely on the internet and technology for its tools, and uses smaller groups of skilled labour to deliver its outputs.

New technologies and the internet have made location less relevant for obtaining work, and the unions have lost a part of their negotiating power as a result. Their members are no longer concentrated in one place and as such the impact of a strike is less effective to their cause. In the case of conflict, employers can move operations to another country with relative ease. Many international companies have installed this type of backup operation in their organisational design, with the aim to become less dependent on unions, single currencies and country legislation.

IS PLATFORM TECHNOLOGY AN OPPORTUNITY FOR NEW FORMS OF COLLECTIVISM?

The rise of the platform economy has generated a renewed interest in some form of representation for independent workers. So far, governments have been reluctant to impose minimum wage levels.

The availability of communication technology can be used by workers to compare information about their working conditions. Tools such as Whatsapp, Facebook and Hustle cater for both independent and employed workers, and provide a means to collect information about pay, coordinate collective demands for improvements through polling, and run world-wide social media campaigns for better treatment.

The ability to collect and share data through new technology, offers opportunities for self-organised groups to gain more insight into work and pay conditions. Companies are increasingly vulnerable to reputational damage when workers use social media for sharing information about poor working conditions or unfair working practices. An example is the recent 'Google Walkout'.[6] Employees in several cities around the world staged protests over the handling of sexual harassment cases where the company had paid millions of dollars in exit packages to male executives accused of misconduct, while staying silent about behaviour transgressions.

Digital communication technology has become an inexpensive way to organise groups, and specific online tools are emerging to service this need. For example, Coworker.org started in 2013 and offers workers functionality to collaborate online to create a document stating their collective demands. It also helps the workers with sharing features on social media platforms, which facilitate the start of a public discussion about work conditions and policies. Another example is Workit, a peer-to-peer smartphone app for Walmart workers where difficult questions about workplace regulations are answered by colleagues. Posts can be anonymous, a feature that protects the whistleblowers. There are other examples, either company-specific or more general initiatives, which all contribute to new forms of collective representation.

ARE UNIONS REPRESENTING INDEPENDENT WORKERS?

The demographics of unions have changed dramatically over time. The average age of union members has gone up as the percentage of membership went down.[7] Younger people feel less inclined to join a union, as they feel a union negotiates mostly on behalf of older members to maintain pension systems, benefits and pay. By giving country-specific examples, we can see early evidence that independent workers are starting to organise themselves through new platforms, or through government, or by joining existing unions.

In the UK, a new union, called the Independent Workers Union, has recently received considerable attention because of its now well known lawsuits against Deliveroo, an online-delivery firm. In the lawsuit the riders claimed they had been unlawfully denied minimum wage and paid holiday. The case centers around the status of independent workers who are active as delivery couriers on Deliveroo's platform. The riders claim they should be treated like employees with the same rights to minimum wages and paid holiday, whereas the company sees the workers as independent, which is the same as self-employed, in which case they do not get the same rights. There are similar lawsuits against Hermes, Uber, Addison Lee, City Sprint, Excel and eCourier, all concerning worker status.[8] In the case of Deliveroo the case was settled out of court and the riders received a sum of money. These lawsuits were funded in a modern, digital way by using crowdfunding and proved to be successful in standing up for those that felt unfairly treated by Deliveroo.

In Germany, ig Metall, allows independent workers to join as a member. Ig Metall is the largest union in Germany and one of its services for independent workers is a website to compare job conditions on different platforms. In Denmark the National Union of Commercial and Clerical Employees has opened a service centre for independent workers.

Traditional unions are finding it increasingly difficult to keep up with new technology developments. A new kind of organisation, which could be referred to as labourtech, can support independent workers with platform technology to create better work and pay conditions outside or inside the traditional unions. A global example would be Mystro, an app for drivers who work on Uber or Lyft. It makes switching between different task providers easy and uses algorithms to analyse different trip requests, making sure the independent workers can select the most profitable trips with the highest ranking customers.

The Netherlands Trade Union Confederation (FNV) has 1.1 million members, making it the largest trade union in the Netherlands. It is still struggling with the question of whether the trade union should stand up for the core of loyal but ageing permanent employees or for the often younger group of independent workers. FNV is organised by sector; for example, FNV Horeca takes care of workers in the hospitality industry. This division has proposed to work together with a fast growing gig-economy company called Temper, which matches supply and demand for independent workers in bars and restaurants. These proposals for joint working are however blocked by FNV's central management, as they are still uncertain about whom to prioritise, employed workers or independent workers.

Given the above, we think it is likely that younger workers will seek to engage with more modern forms of communication and representation. In the next chapter we look at emerging flexible forms of employment and self-employment and look at leading countries and cities where the proportion of independent workers is growing the fastest.

12

THE SWEET SPOT BETWEEN FIX AND FLEX

Subject:
Technology and an open mindset can support labour market flexibility

Key Message
1. The spectrum of employment models across different countries
2. The need for economic policy to close the gap between workers' groups

In this chapter we will closely investigate the opportunities and threats of the platform economy for economic and social stability and how the leading cities and countries organise independent work.

Is flexibility of a country's labour market a threat to economic and social stability or a condition for success? We define independent workers as being self employed, rather than employees, and as providers of services for organisations and individuals. In Chapter 1 we presented research that showed that a large proportion of independent workers follow this model of work out of free choice and that task oriented-work is on the rise, primarily because it is supported by global platform technology developments.

As pointed out in the definition above, the key difference between independent workers and other workers is the absence of an employment contract between the worker and their employer. Employment contracts may be full time or part-time and come in different forms dependent on a country's legal system. They can be set up for a predetermined or indefinite time period.

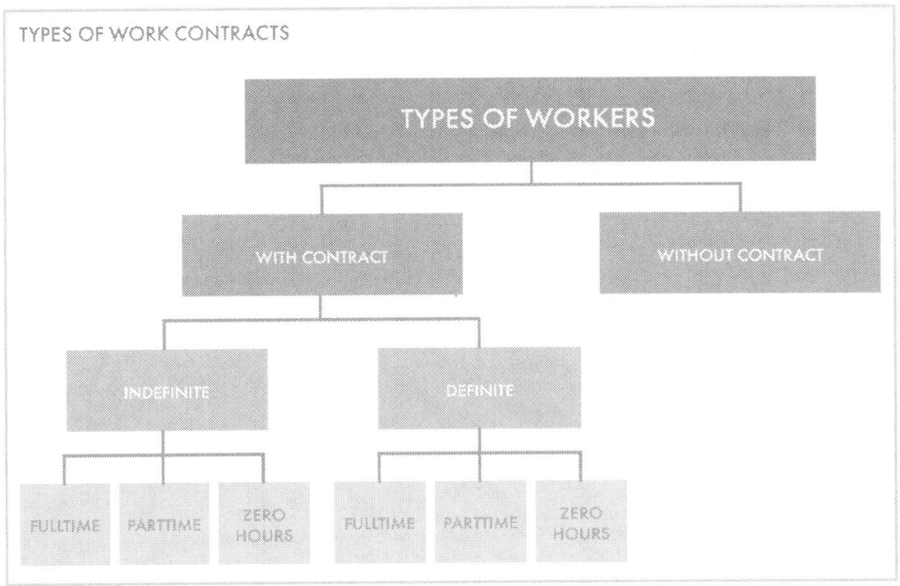

Source: Flex or Fail 2019

There is a strong cultural component to the use of part-time employment contracts. In countries such as France, the Netherlands and Sweden it has become a widely accepted way of employment. In other countries part-time working is almost non-existent.

Part-time employment contracts outline the compensation and benefits for a defined number of hours per day, week or month. Take for example the contract of a maintenance worker, stating that he or she is required to work three defined days per week in return for 60% of a full time salary. In some sectors, such as the hospitality industry, part-time employees will only hear shortly in advance when and for how long they are required to work during a specific week, without the contract defining the minimum of hours. These so-called 'zero-hour contracts' are a source of debate since they might put an employee in a position of risk if he or she is not required to work for a period of time and would thus be deprived of income. Recent changes in UK law have gone some way to address issues regarding zero hour contracts. Employers are obliged to provide workers with details of their rights, such as eligibility to sick leave, level of pay, and maternity leave, on the first day of their engagement.

The table below illustrates the ranking of countries and the percentage of independent work contracts versus temporary contracts.[1]

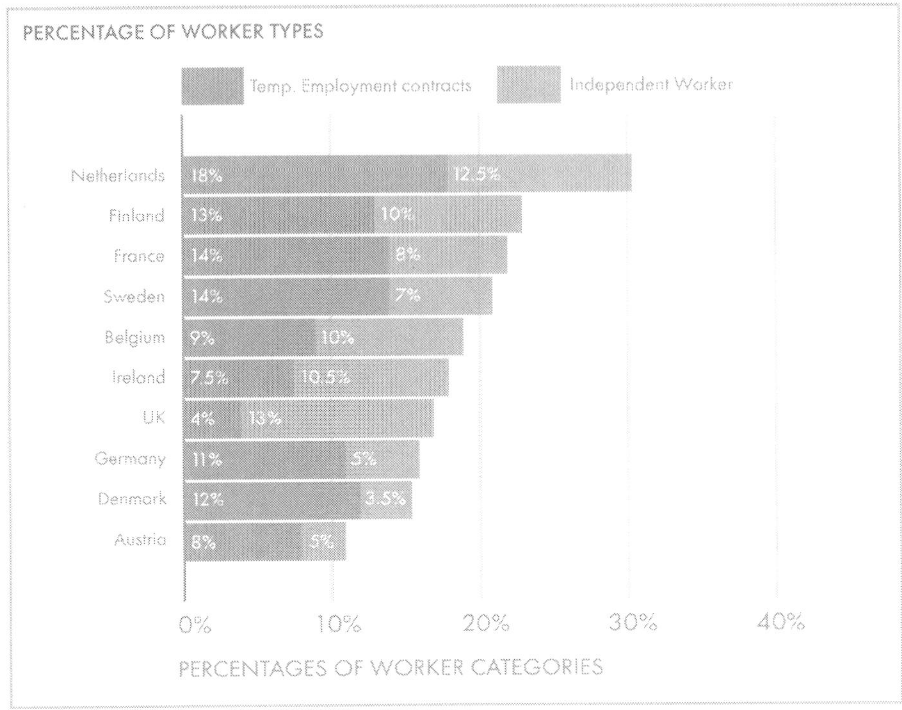

Source: Central Bureau of Statistics, 'Flexwerk in Nederland en de EU', 2017

THE NETHERLANDS' HIGH RANKING

When studying the two figures more closely, one can observe that the Netherlands score high on both contract categories, indicating they have a large proportion of the working population employed part-time. The reason for this high score has to do with a special sort of company that one can find throughout the Netherlands. These companies are called 'temporary worker agencies' or just 'temp agencies', and include companies like Randstad, Adecco or Manpower.

These companies started around the middle of the last century. They provide their clients, who are mostly employers, with workers that can perform certain routine tasks, like loading trucks, reception desk work and packing products. Businesses can request staff for one day of service or a hundred days, depending on the seasonality of their operations. The concept proved successful in many countries around the world, illustrated by the fact that temp agencies (sometimes called staffing companies) are now highly active in well over 40 countries.

In the Netherlands, the demand from employers for part-time workers was at its highest in the 1960's: many women and the elderly who favoured flexible work over full time (re)entered the labour market, something that greatly helped to raise productivity. Politicians in the Netherlands encouraged the growth of temporary contracts, especially when combined with tax deductions that were designed to be favourable to the self-employed.

At the same time, the protection of permanent employees in the Netherlands is greater than elsewhere in the world. It is difficult and expensive for employers to dismiss employees outright, and employees who become ill still need to be paid for up to two years. This has created a tendency amongst employers to create flexible layers within their employment model, which consists mostly of part-time and independent workers. This way, they are able to match supply and demand of labour.

For workers who prefer to work part-time or as an independent worker, it becomes possible to build up a portfolio of different revenue generating activities. An often cited advantage is the variety that this way of working brings. For example, some dentists work two days in a jointly owned practice and combine this with one day of elderly care and 2 days of teaching. According to those interviewed, meeting many different people and being active across different activities reduces the repetition and risk of boredom that could be the result of doing the same thing all week long.

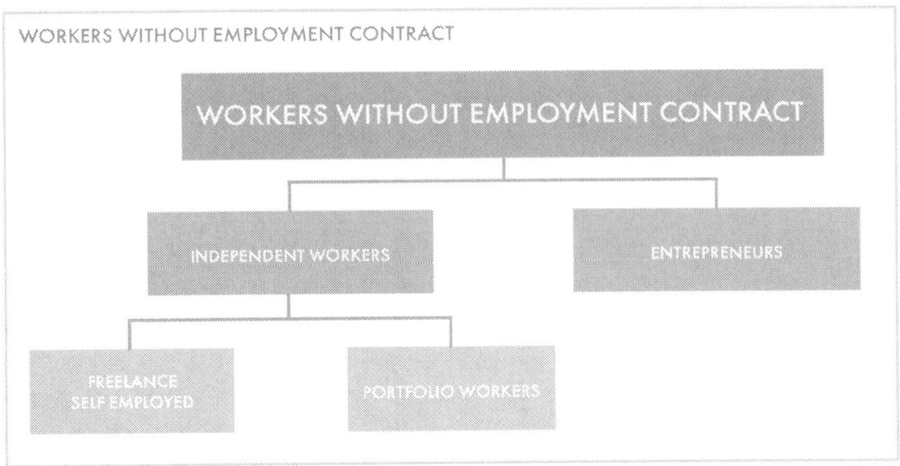

Source: Flex or Fail 2019

Entrepreneurs usually work with higher levels of risk and use specific legal entities, such as a limited liability company, to protect themselves. They take on projects from clients and often coordinate and/or subcontract the work out to others. Independent workers can be seen as self-employed people who perform one project at a time, such as plumbing. Portfolio workers often present themselves with a set of skills or a range of services which they manage themselves.

During the financial crisis of 2008 a large number of people lost their jobs in sectors such as building construction and logistics. When the economy bounced back, many of these workers had already established themselves as independent workers and were not inclined to go back into employment. The degree of autonomy, freedom and tax advantages in combination with their entrepreneurial success created a new class of workers. Surveys show that the majority of self-employed people prefer their independent status over working for a boss, and many workers opt voluntarily for a career as an independent worker.[2]

For an open economy such as The Netherlands, global trade has been the bedrock of economic growth since medieval times and has thrived as globalisation has expanded in recent times. As a result, the Dutch economy of today is in a much better shape than it was thirty years ago, and today's unemployment numbers of around 3.5% are historically low.[3] The country has more than a million independent workers and this group of voters has gained strong political influence.

A recent report by the Economic Board of ING Bank presented two scenarios for the future growth in independent workers.[4] Under the conservative scenario, a further 200,000 people will join the independent workforce. The other scenario describes how an additional 1,000,000 workers could join the ranks of the independents. The impact on the country's social benefit systems, like health insurance and pension funding, would be significant.

ECONOMIC POLICY AND WORKER REPRESENTATION

Think of the labour market as a place where opposing forces are at work. These forces seek either maximum flexibility (and thus competitiveness) or maximum rigidity (in terms of worker protection).

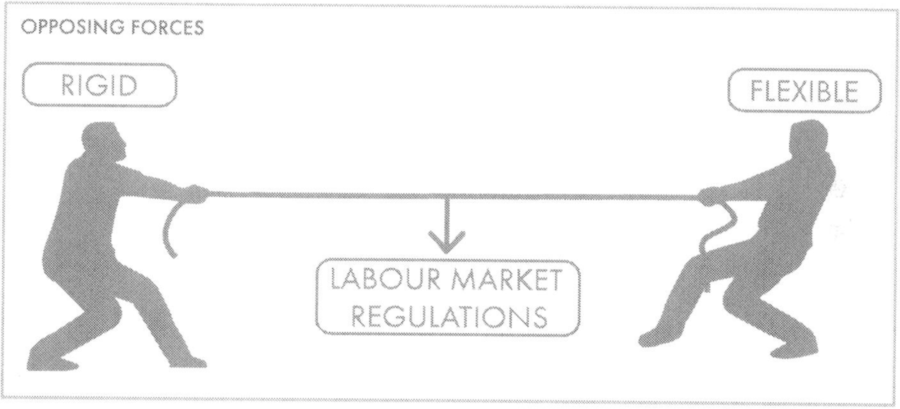

Source: Flex or Fail 2019

One of the forces is the government that is maintaining the competitiveness of the national economy. The opposing forces include the labour unions, who traditionally negotiate compensation and benefits for their members.

The government creates economic policies which regulate taxation, the cost of labour, the incentives (subsidies and taxes) for innovation, the well-being of its citizens, the quality of the education system, the legal system and public infrastructure. In order to keep up with the global economy, individual governments understand that labour market flexibility is important.

The politicians involved in this process realize their voters are engaged in all kinds of work, and carefully balance their desire to remain in power with what the economic policy changes mean for the electorate. So far, most governments have taken a liberal stance towards the platform economy, giving it space to try out new employment opportunities.

The opposing force are the labour unions, who traditionally negotiate compensation and benefits for their members. The unions still have a seat at the negotiating table because of their former performance, but the demographics of their dwindling membership base is steadily shifting towards the 50+ group.

The gap in the middle is steadily increasing. Technology driven platforms aim to take over the role of the temp agency, by matching labour demand and supply directly with algorithms in return for a commission. This is where, in other sectors, Uber, Deliveroo and TaskRabbit realized their growth potential. The risk of 'a race to the bottom' in terms of hourly rates for independent workers is real, but the ability to convert time into money is also attractive to many independent workers.

The IMF and OECD have advocated more flexibility in the labour market for years, but now they are becoming increasingly worried about diminishing worker protection, and the trade-off between competitiveness of markets and inequality. It looks like the pendulum of technologically driven change has swung too far to one side and that some form of adjustment would be appropriate. The next chapter takes us deeper into the world of the independent worker, and how independent workers and organisations can both benefit from new technologies.

13

BACK TO THE FUTURE

Subject:
The platform economy creates opportunities for independent workers

Key Message
1. The rise, fall and rise of the guilds
2. New technologies are creating different forms of organisation

In chapter 1 we described the rise and potential demise of the multinational company, and how the employment model is moving from the security of an employment contract to the uncertainty of independent working. In this chapter we will revisit the history of work from the pre-industrial era to modern times and explore the emergence of the platform economy, and the implications for labour markets.

You might wonder why we first go 'back in time' to try to understand the implications for the future? It was Bob Marley who told us: "if you know your history, then you would know where you're coming from." The sage of Trenchtown was right in this regard: to understand the trajectory of the emerging world of mass independent working, we first need to explore our past. The economy of independent working is not new, it came, went and has returned. History does matter in order to understand the evolution of work and jobs, how technology disruption has affected this in the past and what it tells us about the future.

A SHORT HISTORY OF WORK AND JOBS

The artisan economy of the pre-industrial era was based on people undertaking some form of manual labour especially in agriculture, as well as skilled craftsmen. These craftsman used general purpose tools to make products which required a high degree of customisation and creativity. Skilled craftsmen undertook most of the production steps in the making of the end product themselves to from start to finish.

One feature of skilled work in the pre-industrial era was the formation of guilds, which were associations formed by people who shared certain characteristics and pursued a common purpose, mainly for economic benefit. Guilds go back to the times of ancient Greece and Egypt, but reached their peak in the 1500's. They covered a vast range of workers groups in manufacturing goods and service providers, from shoemakers to physicians, prostitutes to retailers.

The key purpose of guilds was for its members and the political elite of the time to gain economic advantage, including restricting other people from entering their trade or market for services. However, guilds also provided a career path, from training of apprentices, to journeymen and ultimately to mastership. Guilds also supervised and regulated the quality of their goods and services.[1]

By the time that guilds were in decline in the 1700's, the industrial revolution, which started in the 1780's had started and the genesis of the Trade [labour] Unions started to emerge, with the UK being one of the leading countries with regards to such developments. As large numbers of unskilled workers migrated from the countryside to factories and cities in England, collective bargaining began to gather momentum. Although initially repressed by Acts of Parliament in the UK, unions would become established by the 1800's. They were then able to spread to the wider world, with their primary focus on representing their members' interests across a broad range of concerns including pay and working conditions.

While labour unions grew stronger, stressing the importance of working conditions and highlighting the injustice of some of the companies, others were contemplating the theories that lay at the base of such developments in the working world. In 1776, Adam Smith's great work 'The Wealth of Nations' formed the foundation of classical economics. It contributed to a shift in the paradigm of the specialist craftsman to assembly-line production methods driven by the division of labour.

Smith employed examples to illustrate and strengthen his arguments, of which the example of the 'Pin Factory' is one of the most famous. In this case, Smith pointed out that there were 18 steps a specialist worker would need to take to make a pin, an extensive process that resulted in only a handful of pins each week. Smith argued that productivity could be greatly increased if, instead of one man making a complete pin single handedly, an assembly-line manned by a team of people each undertaking one of the 18 individual steps, would transform production to thousands of pins per week. Thus, Smith concluded that the division of labour and worker specialisation drives efficiency and generates prosperity.

Smith's concept opened the way to mass production manufacturing and the drive of workers moving from the countryside to factories in growing towns and cities. By the beginning of the 20th century, the father of 'scientific management' Frederick Winslow Taylor had further refined mass production. He focussed on the principles of enforced standardisation of workers' tasks and the shift of control from workers to management; "under our system, a worker is told just what he has to do, and how he has to do it". Using dedicated manufacturing equipment to produce identical items at low marginal cost became the foundation of modern mass production. However, in doing so, de-skilled workers were now forced to undertake standardised repetitive tasks.

By the mid 20th century, large scale manufacturers saw that, in spite of some obvious benefits like low costs and high productivity, the 'command and control' model of mass production was leading to negative consequences. These included production defects and poor quality, results that had an impact on their brand and customer satisfaction. Toyota was one of the manufacturers whose management decided to combat such negative consequences by refining its production system. They developed more specialised and autonomous teams of workers who could both multi-task and exert control on quality and efficiency of production, including the possibility of stopping the entire production line. Through 'continuous improvement' and reducing defects through 'quality circles', these autonomous teams of workers transformed Toyota's brand and profitability by such an extent that by the late 20th century, principles from the Toyota manufacturing system were being adopted across most manufacturing economies in the developed world. As a consequence, manufacturing workers' skills; autonomy and control started rising.

Since then, demand for skilled workers has steadily risen as economies entered the new millennium. This has accelerated more recently as new technologies based on innovation have replaced traditional mass manufacturing as the driver of economic growth. These technologies require ever higher levels of product and process customisation and thus require workers who are more skilled and flexible, and have knowledge of multiple tasks which they can carry out autonomously, with minimal need of management control. A high level of skills and a high degree of flexibility are once again in fashion and the mantra of the modern era.[2]

WELCOME TO THE PLATFORM ECONOMY

Adam Smith's observations may seem a long way away from the platform economy, but he surely would be impressed by the explosive growth in new companies whose business models promote the sharing of underutilised assets that improve efficiency, sustainability (in terms of using/sharing resources) and community. As part of the platform economy, the sharing economy is based around digital platforms that match buyers with sellers and focuses on utilising idle capacity; the system being based on trust and verification. PwC estimate that the size of the global sharing economy will grow to $335bn by 2025.

As we have described in earlier chapters, the 'gig economy' is also based on digital platforms that connect potential employees with employers who are looking to fill temporary contract based on roles. The temporary contract is thus described as a 'gig'. Reports show that currently in the US, independent workers may comprise up to 35% of the current workforce which is expected to grow to over 50% of the total US workforce by 2027.[3]

Both the sharing and gig economy differ from conventional employment models by their predominant use of independent workers, rather than workers employed on full time or part time employment contracts, however these definitions overlap and may differ across regions and sectors.

What is the driver behind the growth in the gig economy and why does it appear to be displacing the traditional employment model? In the 1930's the economist Ronald Coase postulated that it was more cost effective for firms to employ staff full time and control their activities, than negotiate and enforce separate contracts in the open market for every task.[4] More recently, technology developments have up-ended this theory. Key to this has been the ability of gig economy platforms to identify potential workers with specific skills. The technology matches these workers to the exact task that the organisation requires and, aided by artificial intelligence, is able to select the best match, verify the candidates track record and evaluate the contract fee based on supply and demand.

By more precisely matching labour supply with demand for specific tasks, organisations can optimise their efficiency and cost of labour. In addition, the effective recruitment and monitoring of individual workers performance is likely to increase productivity. Over time, poorly performing workers will less likely be successful in securing work and increasingly be marginalised.

So far, so good, especially for the platform providers, but it may be less good for the individual worker, unless one happens to be a skilled and high performing individual. The gig economy puts less able workers at risk, potentially stripping them of rights to holiday and sick pay and with no pension provision and constant competition for the next job. The lot of the gig worker may become increasingly uncertain and unpleasant.

Yet a Pew Research Centre survey shows a spectrum of opinion about gig working with a majority of respondents agreeing that it was good for people who want flexible schedules, but a minority agreeing with the notion that gig working provides the kind of jobs people can build a career on.

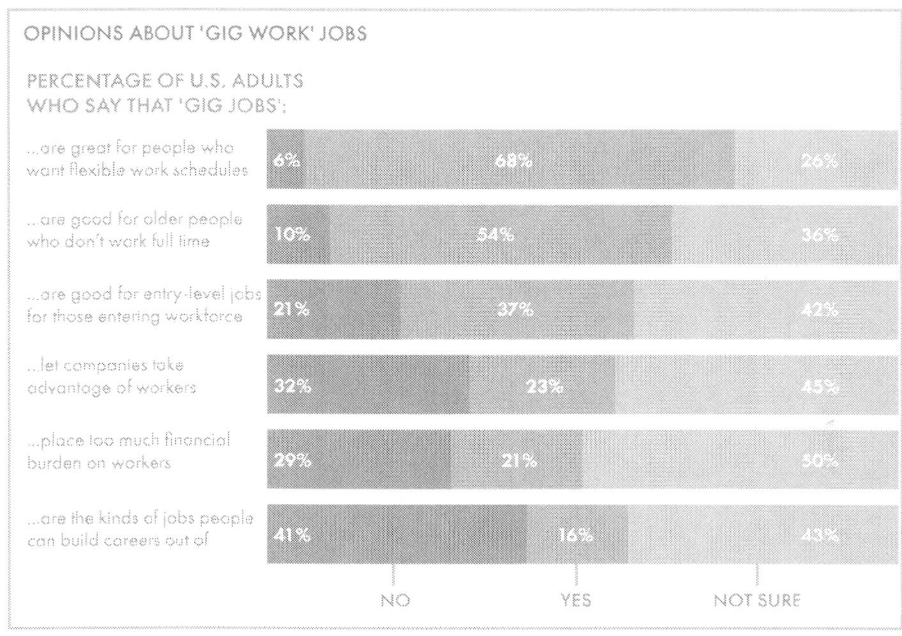

Source: Pew Research Centre

TECHNOLOGY IS EVOLVING FAST

Technology does not stand still, and the sophistication of new technologies will develop at an ever increasing pace. One of those recent developments that will likely impact the labour market significantly is blockchain, a technological development that was first presented to the world in the form of the cryptocurrency Bitcoin.

Blockchain is essentially a digitized, decentralized, public ledger of transactions that allows participants to keep track of transactions without central recordkeeping. Each node (a computer connected to the network) can access the blockchain at any time, looking into the (edited) history that has been performed by other parties on the blockchain, a feature which makes the system completely transparent.

Apart from being the platform on which cryptocurrency such as Bitcoin transactions are conducted, the blockchain has a much greater potential. By developing 'smart contracts' agreed by all parties within a network, a blockchain can allow agreements to be executed automatically, once defined elements within the contract are accomplished. For example, an automated payment can be made as soon as an employee has completed his task, once verified by the blockchain itself. Such a feature has the potential to become pivotal in the work environment, reducing the risk of circulating different versions of contracts and subsequent disputes that may arise. It also improves the cash flow of the independent worker, who does not have to wait several weeks (or sometimes months) before getting paid.

The Distributed Autonomous Organisation or DAO is similar to Bitcoin in that it runs on a blockchain and can be accessed by the nodes that are part of the network. Whereas Bitcoin is accessible to all, a DAO can also be partly accessible to only those who are admitted to that blockchain. As such, a DAO is a complete 'virtual organisation', with its entire business and function built from code. This virtual organisation does not need buildings or managers, but allows people to find each other and reach common goals collaboratively through the formalisation of automated rules. See reference below for more information on this subject in a book called BlockChange, that was co-authored by one of the authors of this book.[5]

How will blockchain impact work in future? The blockchain is capable of offering gig contracts transparently, verifying their execution and authorising payment through smart contracts in an entirely automated way. The transparency of the system, combined with other technologies, is likely to lead to the pay rates for 'easy' gig jobs being lower than the rates for more complex jobs.

Although these emerging technologies may pose a potential threat to some workers, because of its emphasis on the required skills for the offered gigs, its features can also be used to their own advantage. Automated tools such as blockchain could be adopted by labour unions and worker collectives themselves, perhaps even re-creating new forms of guilds that we described earlier on in this chapter. As such, they could develop and use rules built into Smart Contracts to prevent worker exploitation and ensure appropriate payment is made in a timely way. Blockchain could thus become the 'honest broker' or referee that verifies that both teams on the football pitch act according to the rules of the game, that are understood by all parties, without bias or favour.

We can already see some examples of how these developments will probably shape the future of work and pay. Blockchain and other digital technologies are stimulating the emergence of semi-public networks that allow groups of people who are connected to each other to access and utilise the system (provided they have the required permissions). For example, a worker cannot suddenly become a driver for a digital platform taxi hailing firm without going through a vetting process. The same would be true for an online discussion board for doctors or volunteer firefighters. As trust in existing public access digital systems erodes, semi-public networks such as these will grow rapidly.

People who set up and organise new semi-public networks can potentially create great power and value. By forging networks, which may consist of ad hoc groups or permanent teams, they can rapidly generate new business models and social movements, unrestricted by geographical location of its different members and other traditional physical constraints. These networks may even become a new model for 'modern day' guilds by attracting workers who have a common purpose, and creating conditions and benefits collectively that could not be achieved individually.

BUILDING THE FUTURE

We have revisited the past to show how the value of skilled craftsmen gave way to low-skill mass production, and finally returned to high skill autonomous groups that increasingly operate through sophisticated digital platforms to innovate and create value.

The net of the platform economy is spreading far and wide, from crowdfunding to ride hailing services. Whole cities such as Seoul are transforming their growth strategies around the platform economy to create new jobs, economic growth and support for a sustainable society. Bike sharing, car pooling, and sharing enterprise groups are multiplying, all driven by digital platforms through which increasing numbers of participants can engage with.

Over time, economic competitiveness between countries and regions will be increasingly dependent on the effectiveness of their platform economies. Hurdles exist around regulation, taxation, verification and legislation, which lag behind the rapid growth in technology development. However, the race to bring these elements in line with the new digital ecosystem will differentiate winners from losers in terms of gaining competitive advantage.

Smart leaders, be they policy makers, firms or individuals, know this and realise that the future is there to be shaped and grasped. Their goal is not only to secure economic advantage, but also transform the lives of people, communities and the environment. By promoting environmental sustainability through the efficient use of scarce resources, significant benefits to the natural world could be achieved in a cost effective way. Social gains in terms of engagement with communities, bringing people into contact with each other on a local or global scale can also be achieved, a development that encourages social cohesion and reduces inequality.

The future of labour markets will be entwined with these new technologies and tools that support the platform economy. They are there for leaders and individuals to grasp and utilise to their best advantage.

14

THE EMERGING POWER OF ENTREPRENEURSHIP

Subject:
The concept of entrepreneurship influences work & pay

Key Message
1. Entrepreneurship: no return without risk
2. Technology is stimulating entrepreneurship across the board

An entrepreneur is a person who sets up, and takes on the risk for, his or her own business with the expectation of making a profit. A profit enables the entrepreneur to earn a salary and to invest money in the business. They can also retain (some of) the profit to be used later to invest or to pay dividends. When we use the word 'entrepreneur', we generally refer to those individuals who come up with new ideas, take sometimes risky initiatives and, in some cases, end up creating enormous wealth for themselves, like Bill Gates or Mark Zuckerberg. However, it does not have to be this big, entrepreneurs run businesses of many shapes and sizes, from global enterprises to sole traders.

As we have described earlier, by 2025 more than half the working population of developed countries will comprise of independent workers. In order to be successful, these people need some of the skills that an entrepreneur would use to start and run their business. More specifically, independent workers will need these skills sets to establish their enterprise and engage with other workers and clients, or support their own model of independent working. Either way, independent workers take on the risk of managing and organising their own businesses. For that, they need to be adept in creating their own brand and develop effective networks that support their new way of working. A quiet revolution will need to take place that over time creates an army of 'personal entrepreneurs', who apply the key principles of a risk taking entrepreneur in order to transition to become an independent worker, and achieve their personal financial goals. This chapter will take a closer look at what risks people take to transition towards becoming an independent worker, and the skills and strategies that they will need to develop to achieve success.

THE GROWTH OF ENTREPRENEURSHIP IN AN ERA OF DIGITAL DISRUPTION

In previous chapters we have seen that automation might replace 15% of workers by 2030[1], but in spite of this, a high demand for workers with specific skills will continue. Although many categories of work will be replaced by automation, many will not, and demand for new types of jobs will emerge.

Each new era of automation impacts jobs that involve more complex tasks, so while demand for workers, who now spend their time processing data or undertake predictable physical tasks may decline, demand for innovators, team coordinators and tech designers will increase. Many of these skilled new workers will be professionally active in novel ways and as such evolve to become 'independent workers'.

Research shows that digital technologies will not just disrupt certain work areas, but it will also disrupt the process by with entrepreneurs will operate, including how they innovate as well as how they finance, grow and deliver their businesses. For example, business models are changing rapidly, with digitisation of how products and services are designed, customised and delivered directly to customers, by-passing traditional intermediaries. Access to the sharing economy is monetising underutilised assets and digital platforms are driving value creation from closer customer relationships and stimulating innovation around new products and services. Business models that are based on impact and outcomes are rapidly replacing established 'activity and input' type models. This type of business model disruption will also enable independent workers to enter new markets in a more agile way which will give them competitive advantage over incumbents.

What factors make an entrepreneur successful? Stories of an individual entrepreneur's personal journey from 'rags to riches' stimulate such dreams for many people. However, as with many things, the reality of such ventures is far more complex and risky. Research suggests that around 90% of business in the US that are started by entrepreneurs fail in the first five years. Nevertheless some 23 million small businesses exist in the US alone.[2]

There are many factors required to become the new Bill Gates, of which luck and timing play a large role. More concrete success factors that are highlighted in research include: past experience, a strong vision and business concept as well as effective planning and execution. Most early stage entrepreneurs suffer from one or more 'near death experiences' such as running out of cash or failing to secure adequate sales. The adage 'what doesn't kill you makes you stronger' can be applied to those who survive these challenges.

Apart from the skills an entrepreneur must develop, having a mentor and effective networks are vital to guide and support the independent worker. A mentor can assist the entrepreneur during the phase of growth, where the skills and training needed to develop leadership, vision and an effective growth strategy become more important. Gaining access to necessary capital, protecting intellectual property, and managing cash flow are fundamental activities at all stages.

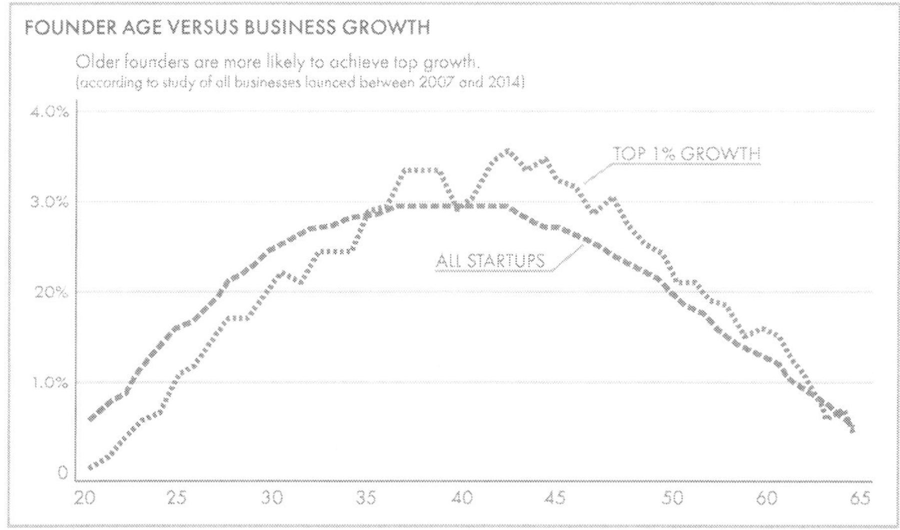

Source: The Conversation. Source Pierre Azoulay, Benjamin F. Jones, J. Daniel Kim and Javier Miranda

As younger people enter the workforce and employed people look for a change of direction in their careers, new entrepreneurs are emerging across the demographic spectrum. In spite of younger entrepreneurs being native users of digital technology, an analysis of businesses in the US found that older investors were actually more successful as entrepreneurs, with the under 25's performing badly as a consequence of lacking experience and financial resources.

Above the age of 25 however, younger entrepreneurs have the advantage of being able to capitalise on digital tools and technologies while also understanding the potential for innovation. In many countries, high levels of youth unemployment are spurring younger people to follow an entrepreneurial career and build job-creating businesses. This phenomenon is likely to grow as networks and clusters, such as start-up incubators and technology transfer offices in universities, develop and mature.

Mid-career and older workers have been switching to become entrepreneurs in rising numbers over the last 10 years in the US, with the 55-64 demographic growing the fastest. Older workers generally have the advantage of more experience with a higher level of knowledge and skills, as well as industry expertise, which is correlated to higher levels of entrepreneurial success. Their access to own money and 'human capital' gives this demographic group many advantages in terms of exploiting potential opportunities and executing plans more successfully.

Female entrepreneurs are an especially interesting and changing demographic to take a look at, because they are an upcoming and rapidly expanding segment. Historically, in developed countries, men have been more likely to become entrepreneurs than women. In the UK, the ratio was observed to be as extreme as 2 to 1, with a defined 'gender enterprise gap'. In developing countries the picture is different with countries such as Ecuador having only 32% of women of working age described as 'entrepreneurs'. There are various reasons for this historical bias including cultural factors, limited access to capital and responsibility for unpaid caring roles, which is also likely to make women more risk averse. However, this situation is changing, with more women choosing to be entrepreneurs. Evidence shows that women who strive for a more flexible lifestyle, and want to retain control over their work, are opting to start their own businesses. The growth rate of new businesses started by women is now actually outpacing those started by men in some developed economies.

Lumping entrepreneurs into a single category of profit seeking individuals, regardless of the demographic group they belong to, would be a false characterisation. The growth of not-for-profit social enterprises are an important part of this movement and include individuals who aim to develop innovative solutions to societal challenges including social, environmental and cultural, though start-up companies or other organisations.

Appealing particularly to the younger demographic, social entrepreneurs are looking for promising results from their effort in terms of societal impact, such as alleviating poverty or creating environmental benefits. Often working in collaboration with other organisations, social entrepreneurs are driven by their values and increasingly tap into crowdfunding sources of capital through connection with people who share similar values and beliefs. Social entrepreneurs will represent an increasing segment of the independent workforce, especially since this group will mainly concern the younger, 'just starting' generation. This segment might also include hybrid forms of this model, as individuals seek more authentic forms of reward from work and purpose for their lives. They can be independent workers, creating their own working environment, by joining networks with the same values and looking for work with impact on aspects that they themselves find important.

WELCOME TO 'BRAND CALLED YOU!'

Entrepreneurs who establish businesses that involve marketing and selling products or services generally invest time and resources in building a brand identity for their enterprises. But how does this relate to people who are transitioning to independent working for the first time? How do they brand and distinguish themselves as individuals in a competitive market? As the management guru Tom Peters pointed out in 1997 "we are all CEO's of our own company, Me Inc.!", and we find much truth in his words.

For first time independent workers, marketing oneself is a key part of launching a career and projecting this to key stakeholders in a positive way. Branding experts suggest that this task starts with defining 'who you are and who you are not,' after which one can start to build such a brand identity and reputation around that definition. Strong personal brands need to be managed effectively through multiple channels across both online and offline platforms. In order to differentiate oneself in a noisy marketing environment, a personal entrepreneur needs to reflect on multiple things at once, and not just on what services to provide. One should at the same time think about values, authenticity and personality in order to engage with audiences impactfully.

Projecting an effective personal brand goes beyond different media platforms and must also be deployed in every day personal engagements. It is important to create a presence within the target market audience that the entrepreneur seeks to engage and influence. As such, active networking is vital to entrepreneurial success.

Research evidence demonstrates that informal professional networks and communities are more important for entrepreneurial success than formal structures such as start-up business incubators and accelerators.[3] The findings show that active networking had a positive impact on their businesses; it shows a strong relationship between the level of active networking and metrics of business success. Both online and physical networking activities were seen to be complementary.

Networking clearly provides many potential benefits for all forms of independent working, including: market information, sales leads, mentoring and recruitment opportunities. This is especially true for those people just starting out in independent working and who often work alone. Research shows that finding the right networks to engage is not straightforward, even with the help of the internet. The majority of the entrepreneurs surveyed still found access to informal communities through word-of-mouth sources, however this differed somewhat between countries.

DEVELOPING AN ENVIRONMENT FOR ENTREPRENEURSHIP TO THRIVE

In 1964, concerns over how the US economy might adapt to a period of rapidly advancing technology and automation prompted the then President Lyndon Johnson to sign into law a National Commission on Technology, automation and Economic Progress which contained the following passage in its final report:

> *"...but the general level of demand for goods and services is by far the most important factor determining how many are affected [by unemployment], how long they stay unemployed, and how hard it is for new entrants to the labour market to find jobs. The basic fact is that technology eliminates jobs, not work. It is the continuous obligation of economic policy to match increases in productive potential with increases in purchasing power and demand. Otherwise the potential created by technical progress runs to waste in idle capacity, unemployment, and deprivation."*[4]

Clearly time has moved on; we face a different global economic environment and advances in technology than Lyndon Johnson did in 1964. Nevertheless governments and policy makers are pivotal in shaping economic policy that can stimulate productivity growth, which is directly linked to employment over the long term.

Governments can greatly influence the process of how skill levels of workers can be upgraded to meet future needs. This especially applies to mid-career workers who may have missed out in training around use and application of new technologies, training that is crucial in the current transition to even more technology-driven economies. Current education and training models in many developed economies are backward facing and need revision, if they are to be fit for purpose to equip workers for this era of automation. Some experts in the US believe that in spite of 10 years of education that children now receive, they are not taught how to transfer that knowledge to the 'real world'. This often results in a poor career choice, and a lack of skills needed for a job they would really enjoy.[5]

Governments can provide transitional support to workers whose industry sectors are contracting, due to automation or other technology disruption. They can also provide support for developing short term financial support, tax breaks for training and lifelong learning, formation of networks and incubators for new start-ups and expert support and mentoring through academic and professional networks.

Taxation, access to capital and entitlement to core benefits such as income support also need reform in order to meet the needs of cohorts of workers who are transitioning to independent forms of work from more secure employment contracts. Governments prefer tax collection through the payroll of companies, as it gives the tax authorities more control. It is much more difficult to collect tax and social benefits from independent workers, which may cause resistance at governmental level to change current practices. Finally, governments need to improve the collection and analysis of data regarding independent working in order to better understand changing labour dynamics that will inform smart policy interventions.

Artificial intelligence, machine learning and the previously discussed blockchain are some of the technologies that potentially have the power to accelerate economic growth and as such, should to be viewed as an opportunity more than a threat. They will however disrupt traditional employment models in certain sectors and pose a threat to large numbers of jobs in the short to medium term.

New skills will be in demand, especially in growth sectors such as technology, infrastructure, renewable energy and healthcare. The number of people transitioning to independent working will rise and address some of the demand for these new roles. By embracing independent working, many workers will thrive, and as a consequence live fulfilling lives, but this requires a new way of working that will not happen by default. Organisations and policymakers need to make bold steps to make sure the economic benefits of these changes encompass the many, not just a few who by their own efforts, networks and luck, will achieve success.

15

CREATING MULTIPLE INCOME STREAMS

Subject:
Diversification of income streams reduces your risk

Key Message
1. There are two kinds of income streams: passive and active
2. Stick to the day job when you start, but add additional income streams

According to financial advisors, having six months of savings available is a prudent strategy, should some unexpected financial emergency befall you or your family. For those living in a metropolitan area in the US, those savings would equate to around $23,000, but a recent survey showed that 57% of US adults at any time have less than $1,000 available.[1] At the other end of the scale, research studies have identified that people with a net asset wealth of more than a million dollars have on average seven different income streams, although we well recognise that this may reflect a degree of 'cause and effect'.[2] How might those people with minimal savings go about generating more income streams?

In an era of increasing digital disruption, risks to individuals' jobs and uncertainty of future income from a salary are both increasing. This potentially affects all demographic groups and skill levels. A key defence strategy for protecting those people whose income is coming solely from one particular salary includes income diversification. As could be observed with the numbers described above, the most wealthy group in the US has a shared characteristic of having multiple incomes. This chapter looks at why multiple income streams are increasingly important, what sources these come from and how individuals can diversify as income from a salary becomes less certain in an age of automation.

WHY MULTIPLE INCOME STREAMS ARE IMPORTANT

'Don't put all your eggs in one basket', as the old saying goes. Classic portfolio theory tells us that owning different kinds of financial assets is less risky than owning just one type. The key insight behind this theory is that a single asset's risk and return should not be assessed by itself, but by how it contributes to a portfolio's overall risk and return. This approach has become the background to investment strategy ever since it was first described by Harry Markowitz in 1952. There is some logic in applying portfolio investment theory to personal income planning. Although this might sound complicated, it comes down to an intuitive logic: having multiple income streams is likely to increase resilience and promote the ability to recover from a misfortune over having a single one. Having diversification of income streams may therefore lower risk that comes from an increasingly uncertain work environment.

Throughout the book we have highlighted the likelihood of the rapid transition over the next decade from employment to independent working in general, but also to look at the actual effects and changes in pay. In developed countries, the majority of people with an employment contract currently rely on a weekly or monthly salary for income needed to live and pay the bills. Many workers spend five years or less in their jobs, and shorter periods in defined work would automatically lead to devoting more time and energy needed for the transition from one job to another. In January 2016, the US Bureau of Labour statistics reported the average employee tenure was 4.2 years, a decrease compared to 4.6 years in January 2014. To add to this increasing risk, personal savings rates in the US [defined as the ratio of personal income saved to personal net disposable income, which is defined as the amount of money that households have available for spending and saving after income taxes have been accounted for] have halved over the last 50 years.

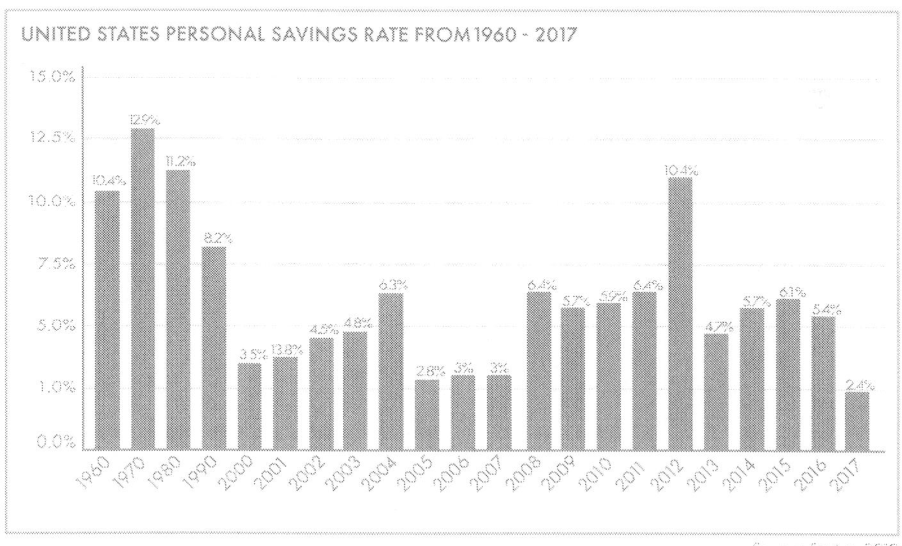

Source: Statista 2019

The data points to an increasing risk to many in society, especially for certain demographic groups such as the young and women, who have lower levels of savings and work in lower paid jobs. More frequent gaps between employment and low levels of savings put individuals and their dependents at increasing risk.

Multiple income sources are not new and across history, and across all economies, people have supplemented incomes by doing additional jobs 'on the side' and generate income from multiple forms of enterprise. In the US, roughly 42% of men and 30% of women report that they already have multiple streams of income.[3] However, it appears that many of these people are not completely aware of the multiple incomes themselves, nor formalise their income streams into a diversified strategy that protects them from risk. One obvious example to illustrate this is that most households already have a second salary or income from a spouse or partner which brings in income diversity. However, even this example should be interpreted with some caution, as both workers could share the same employer or work in the same sector.

Experiencing an impactful life event, high levels of stress or just getting older is often a prompt for many people to re-evaluate their work-life balance. This can stimulate reflection on their cost of living, which leads them to either downsize or re-allocate their spending. Resetting personal priorities and goals are often coupled with a review of financial needs and alternative ways of living and generating income. With life expectancy rising in most developed economies, around 50% of 85 year olds say that they are 'still able to work'.[4] As the workforce ages, some job activities become increasingly difficult to be carried out, for example heavy manual work and flying airplanes. Workers in these particular professions would be well advised to develop multiple income streams early on in their careers.

WHERE DO MULTIPLE INCOME STREAMS COME FROM?

As we have seen in an earlier chapter, management consultancy McKinsey identifies four categories of independent workers of whom casual workers are described as 'workers using independent work for supplemental income and who do so by choice'. Some of these have traditional jobs, others are students, retirees or caregivers.[5] It could include a teacher who keeps bees as a hobby and sells honey, or a care worker who sells used items on eBay. These 'casual workers' were found to have higher levels of satisfaction than those who solely hold traditional jobs.

Reviewing household spending categories may identify resources that can be saved, so that these can be used as a means to create new sources of income. By focusing on their primary salary as a means to maximise cash flow, individuals may have further scope to invest in secondary income streams, such as starting a business or investing, individually or collectively, in property with the savings from current expenditures.

Multiple income streams can be divided into 'active' and 'passive' forms. Passive forms are income streams that, apart from initial set up or creation, do not directly take up time related to generate income, but instead continue to run in the background with some oversight. Examples include income from renting property or assets, royalties from book or music publishing, licensing from product development and investment income. Active income streams on the other hand are related to direct time and effort, needed to generate such income. These forms of income include: earned income from employment, business income and independent working.

Although people have developed multiple income streams throughout history, the emergence of digital platforms have been transformative in both reach and accessibility. McKinsey identified that independent workers in the US and EU-15 who sell goods or lease assets are more likely to use digital platforms [63% and

36% respectively] than those who just provide labour [6%]. Newly developed technologies are contributing to an expansion of independent working that is growing both the scope and scale of earning activities that can benefit independent workers.

Digital platforms are also transforming the way in which people can access investment opportunities that previously were inaccessible without considerable capital outlay. For example, in order to acquire a rental property, a down payment of 20% of the full price is often required, which is beyond the means of many people. This has been transformed by crowdfunding through platforms like FundRise who provide access to fractional ownership of real estate from $5,000 onwards.[6]

The fact that millionaires appear to have an average of seven separate income streams, as mentioned at the start of this chapter does however not directly imply that seven is the magic number or indeed, that having diverse income streams is the road to riches. On the contrary, it is important to realise that for most people, multiple income streams take time and skill to develop and consume an individual's effort and resources. People embark on this course for a variety for reasons: to keep their 'head above water' if they need more income, to gain greater control over their work-life balance or just to monetise their hobby, which can be rewarding. Going forwards, the predominant driver for income diversification will be around managing personal risk from the threat of existing jobs being supplanted by automation and technology.

HOW TO MANAGE INCOME DIVERSIFICATION

Developing multiple income streams may start in a small way and build up over time. By sticking to a day job, motivated people can for example find time in the evenings or weekends to start a new online micro business or rent out a room through an online platform. With good luck and planning, this could expand over time to become more and more of a portfolio working model. The idea is to take money one earns from work and invest a portion of this into assets that generate a return which can support further diversification. Consequently, this would strengthen an individual's resilience to keep going and fill an income gap, should one source of income fall out or fail entirely.

Although this sounds easy, in reality careful research and planning is required. Unless you have the necessary skills from the start, advice and guidance during the process of setting up multiple income streams is crucial in order to avoid mistakes, especially when investing in more capital intensive opportunities. In chapter 14 we alluded to the importance of seeking out networks and building a personalised brand. These activities are pertinent to developing multiple income streams.

Like some aspects of portfolio working, which we will expand on in chapter 16, people who successfully develop multiple streams of income have a high degree of autonomy, can cope with uncertainty and operate in a working environment outside any single organisation. Naturally they can also face risks that most independent workers are exposed to, such as not getting paid for work delivered and missing out on pension and sick pay benefits.

Whether you create websites or keep bees to sell honey as a way of creating additional incomes streams, you will need to keep up your skills and operate your businesses efficiently in order to avoid such risks. Your rewards will be the satisfaction that comes from autonomy and freedom plus work that you can control, as well as gaining resilience from diversified income streams needed to protect you from future uncertainty.

16

SKILLS AND ATTITUDES REQUIRED FOR A PORTFOLIO APPROACH

Subject:
Why the portfolio approach is becoming increasingly attractive

Key Message
1. Planning for multiple income streams
2. Managing multiple activities simultaneously

WHAT IS A PORTFOLIO APPROACH?

A portfolio approach is a term that is defined as having several professional activities at the same time rather than a single full time job, and may form part of a 'multiple income stream' strategy. Will most people develop a portfolio approach at some point in their live? How does this happen in practice and what will this mean for society?

The number of people who are following the path of portfolio working has accelerated substantially in recent years. This is not only triggered by people's desire to work outside a traditional employment contract. As we have described earlier in this book, the emergence of digital platforms has created markets between buyers and sellers of services, enabling transactions in a low cost and efficient manner, which would not have been possible previously.

The portfolio approach is used by a wide spectrum of people, some of whom are fully independent, running their own business, while also undertaking part time employed roles or an unpaid role in the voluntary sector. Individuals may have a mix of assured income streams, as well as more speculative or entrepreneurial roles generating little or no income.

DRIVERS TO ADOPT A PORTFOLIO APPROACH

What makes people give up the security of a full time job that is underpinned by an employment contract? Clearly there are a variety of circumstances surrounding those that make this shift, and it is something that can happen either by choice or involuntarily. As we highlighted in Chapter 1, around 30% of people who follow a portfolio approach do so by necessity; precipitated by job loss, a period of illness, childcare, elder care and so on. The remaining 70% choose to have a portfolio of activities and explain this by saying they have a desire to do something more fulfilling, a chance to change direction in life or, they want to reduce stress.

However most of all, they simply want to gain autonomy over their working lives, with more self-determination, creativity and an overall better lifestyle.

At the older end of the scale, labour market participation in the 50-65 age group in the UK has risen steadily over the last 25 years and, more notably, the participation of the over 65's has doubled in the last decade, with around 50% of these undertaking independent and portfolio work. As defined benefit pensions decline and individuals live longer, this rise in portfolio working into older age is likely to continue to increase.

Meet Nancy, she is a divorced woman of 52 with two grown up children at college and one daughter of 17 who is at school and lives with her at home. Nancy took the decision to follow a portfolio approach around two years ago:

"I had been a teacher in a secondary school for around five years and headed up a department, as well as teaching full time. I loved my job but it had become increasingly difficult to manage with more and more bureaucracy, reports and regulations to deal with. Preparing for classes, marking work, meeting with parents and managing staff all began to take a toll on me, both physically and psychologically.

I guess the tipping point for me was that my daughter began to have some mental health problems and this required more of my time to support her through a difficult period. All of this got on top of me and I became quite stressed. I knew something had to give and after discussing it with friends and colleagues I had the idea that I would give up teaching full time and move to some different way of working.

I thought I would just work as a part time teacher and that would allow me to spend more time supporting my daughter and get my own life back together. I told the school that I was going to resign my full time role, but they were really upset and said they wanted me to stay on somehow. We finally agreed that I would teach for three mornings a week, and focus on kids with a high level of needs who required more of a 'one to one' approach.

I was obviously worried about money, I live alone with my daughter and have a big mortgage on my apartment. I needed more income than just a couple of mornings teaching. I have a spare room in my apartment and managed to find a lodger who was going through a divorce and wanted to rent a room. It works really well and the money helps a lot.

Following giving up full time work, I joined an agency that provides temporary teaching staff to schools. I didn't really like this work but it paid quite well and at least it was flexible around my needs to support my daughter. During that time I was approached by someone who wanted their children home schooled and asked me whether I could help in teaching them at home. I gave up the temp job and now have a small business that teaches kids at home. More recently, I was asked to do some editing work for a magazine, and now have more work than I can really manage alone, so I farm some of it out to other colleagues and charge a small profit margin on their work.

Overall, in the two years since I gave up teaching, I have worked hard to make a go of it independently. I have had loads of help from friends and colleagues as well as my clients who I think value my work. All of this has helped in getting new work in. With my four current income streams I am earning in total more than I was when I was a full time teacher. I'm not saying it is easy to keep all these different things going, but I am in control of my work and feel I can support my daughter properly. She is gradually improving as well. That is a great relief to me."

Clearly no two people are alike and Nancy's story as to how she transitioned from fulltime work to becoming a portfolio worker is shaped by her unique circumstances. Yet this account is common to a lot of people whose lives change in unexpected ways that forces them to re-evaluate their style of work in order to manage other aspects of their life.

Nancy clearly made some effort to plan this transition, and took advice from other people. She had the advantage of having a professional skill, teaching, and using her reputation and network to find new forms of work. She also exploited her unused assets by renting out a room. Without knowing it, she had started a new portfolio activity.

IMPACT OF THE PORTFOLIO REVOLUTION ON THE WORKFORCE AND OTHER STAKEHOLDERS

If the 'new normal' of work is a portfolio approach, significant changes need to take place to skill and equip individuals to succeed and thrive in this new environment. Like all forms of independent working, developing business skills, creating a personal brand and a compelling web presence are key success factors for managing a portfolio. Much of portfolio working revolves around building successful networks and having support from mentors to guide and challenge decision-making. The adage to 'not give up the day job before you have secured your first piece of work' may be a good mantra to those who underestimate the transition between full time work and portfolio activities.

From an economic perspective, portfolio working may offer a route to re-engage in the labour market for those who are unemployed or have left employment for personal circumstances, such as childcare. This option allows greater flexibility, adaption and tailored entry that may be more preferable to an employment model. As such, portfolio working may produce significant economic benefits with employers having access to a larger workforce market, and a part of society potentially being less dependent on state benefits. However, this is clearly balanced by the need for the state and other organisations to provide necessary support, skills and services that enable individuals to take advantage of this growing opportunity. This support may include grants to pay for training courses and access to specialist advisors.

MANAGING RISK AND FINANCIAL PLANNING

Without the reliance of an assured weekly or monthly paycheck, all independent workers are on their own in terms of managing income and survival. This is a daunting task, especially for those without existing financial resources or those who have people depending on them. Many people who transition from employment to independent working will earn more money than they did previously, although this may take some time to build up. For others, they will never achieve the same level of income as they did when employed, either by choice, or through lack of demand for their independent worker skills.

The uncertainty and often short term nature of portfolio working makes financial planning and management essential, starting with a clear understanding of one's own financial requirements and income needs. The transition to portfolio working begins with developing a personal financial plan as part of a larger business plan or indeed 'life plan'; mapping out these overall personal objectives is a worthwhile exercise.

Clearly, the portfolio approach covers a broad range of individuals with very different financial needs. A 55 year old with 20 years of senior corporate experience and a substantial pension may be more relaxed in the approach to maximising income, favouring a range of activities based on conviction or personal interest, some of which may be unremunerated. For others however, especially those 30% who choose a portfolio strategy by necessity, income maximisation is key, and as such will be more focussed on higher paying and more secure income streams.

Developing a 'balanced portfolio' of income streams has similarities to managing an investment portfolio. There will be a spectrum of risk and return that needs managing, as well as balancing the amount of effort and time spent on each income generating enterprise. Looking at the portfolio approach in this way provides a useful model for allocating resources to deliver optimal returns, which may be both financial and non-financial in nature, depending on personal preference.

When developing a portfolio approach, people should consider their whole spectrum of assets, also those that go beyond their personal labour. Their assets, including property, may form an important part of their overall portfolio. Mapping out each potential income source from services, goods and assets forms the basis of the plan. Costs would then be applied and contingency around timing and uncertainties should be built into the model. The plan would evolve over time and become fine-tuned as more real world experience is taken into account and included into the model.

Understanding the key risks that arise from transitioning to the portfolio approach is naturally very important in order to mitigate uncertainties. Common feedback from people new to this form of income generation includes the warning to carefully consider cash flow management, especially because there are often delays in getting paid by customers. You can imagine that a 90 day delay from completing a job to getting paid may be a 'killer blow' to someone naïve to independent working and with minimal financial reserves.

A careful analysis of risk and mitigating actions such as taking out insurance for sickness or building up multiple income streams that create resilience is also crucial. Developing an inventory of potential risks and ranking these, enables a more analytical approach to contingency planning.

A significant percentage of people embarking on a portfolio approach will have a partner who may be working or who they may collaborate with on some aspects of their work. This provides support in multiple ways, such as additional resource, augmenting skills and alleviating the solitude of lone working. It therefore needs to be considered in the planning process as it can make a great difference.

Longer term planning for retirement and ensuring adequate pension arrangements are as important for people who follow the portfolio approach as for the employed worker and would also need to be factored into the individual's overall 'life plan'. One can devise a plan for the short term and be completely content with that, but if the long term is forgotten, difficulties arise at an older age, which cannot easily be reversed.

INTEGRATING PORTFOLIO WORK AND LIFE

For the majority of people, the decision to follow this path is often prompted by a desire to rebalance work and life, and develop in new directions following a period of employment. Words such as 'greater autonomy', 'creativity', 'personal fulfillment' and 'giving something back' were often used as a reason by individuals we engaged with while researching this book on transitioning to portfolio working.

In reality, the opposite is sometimes the case. Independent working is generally being stripped of the support that is normally provided by a full time employer. Finding and delivering work to multiple clients, time management, administration, financial management, filing tax returns etc. often invade evenings, weekends and up-end holiday plans. Loneliness is a common issue for people who are used to regular social engagement with work colleagues and as independents, often work from home on their own. For many, loneliness can sap motivation and lead to anxiety and depression, especially when the going gets tough.

Having support networks, a social infrastructure, and a mentor can support the lone worker transitioning from a more structured working environment and are therefore important strategies needed to sustain a more independent way of working.

Disciplined time management and being well organised are the by-words for people who follow the portfolio approach. Making space for leisure, exercise, sleep and relationships is of fundamental importance to mental and physical good health. Effective and experienced portfolio practitioners seem able to keep a lot of 'balls in the air' while also enjoying a good quality of life and achieving their desired level of income. This usually takes some years to perfect as an art but most individuals we interviewed believed that the personal journey they had undertaken was worthwhile and would not go back to an employed role.

Our understanding of the economic drivers and consequences of this trend will become clearer over time. So far, the personal stories we have explored in this book reveal a spectrum of outcomes that overall point to a sense of optimism. We believe that this will increase over time as conditions, systems, technologies and skills improve to support what may become a dominant model of work. In part three of the book, we will look at the output of independent working and how this impacts quality of life.

PART 3

PERSONAL JOURNEYS

17

HAPPINESS VERSUS MEANINGFUL

Subject:
There is a difference between 'being happy' and 'living a meaningful life'

Key Message

1. Becoming independent means leaving behind the social aspects of work
2. Treat your well being with as much attention as your work

Albert Einstein said "Not everything that can be counted counts, and not everything that counts can be counted", a statement we apply to the phenomenon of happiness in the context of money in this chapter.

Why does the subject of happiness appear in a book that is centered around the changing job market and the trend towards independent work? We think that happiness is an important factor to consider when exploring the future of work and pay, as the three are intertwined. Contrary to what many might believe, research shows that money contributes to happiness up to a certain extent, but that more money beyond that point does not necessarily increase a person's happiness. For some people, as we will see, more time or autonomy would contribute to a higher level of happiness.

Gross National Happiness (GNH) is, for example, taken seriously by the government of Bhutan. GNH is an index which is used to measure the collective happiness and well-being of the population, and the government of Bhutan sets specific goals around the metrics. The index was developed by the Centre for Bhutan Studies with the help of researchers from Oxford University to help measure the progress of Bhutanese society. There has been some criticism that the measurement is being used to disguise the country's poverty level, which is something to keep in mind.

One of the themes of this book is to clarify the many elements that generate value for someone working independently. Much of this has little to do with money, as life can be much less costly when one takes a close look at status-related spending. Happiness has become a major topic in social science, where artists, philosophers and social scientists agree that happiness has multiple dimensions.[1] In this chapter we take a closer look at happiness and its relation to leading a meaningful life.

An important, fundamental question that we first have to ask ourselves is what makes people happy? We do not claim to have the final answer to this question, and do not offer a simple formula. It's a topic which we would like to approach cautiously and with humility. We can start by saying the 'happiness can also be the absence of sadness or disaster' in a person's life.

Being alive, healthy, entertained, working, living in a good country or city and in possession of an education are very precious attributes and highly contributory factors. Happiness is also personal and unique; some people value everyday items such as a short commute to work or safe cycling routes to work more than others. General factors, such as access to nature, clean air, good quality water and safety are elements that are considered of real value to most people, since those are basic requirements to live a happy and healthy life. These last elements might seem to be free of cost, but are they really? Clearly, there are costs involved in keeping the environment green and clean. These costs should be taken into account when measuring economic progress and indeed accounting for natural capital is becoming an increasingly important subject in economics.

Happiness has both an emotional and a cognitive side. Feelings of a state of well-being which are associated with happiness include feeling safe, being comfortable, elated, joyful, proud and delighted. Unhappiness includes feelings such as worry, anger and sadness. Apart from the direct association between experiencing such feelings and happiness, there is the more indirect influence on happiness which involves people's reflections on how they live. These evaluations are difficult to measure objectively as people's memories are unreliable at best. Even the most simple of experiences like the amount of sunshine, being hungry or events prior to the measurement, such as having lost some loose cash from your pockets on a train, can all hugely influence the evaluation of happiness. In social sciences the average of the results of the two different measurements of happiness is usually taken, in order to reach the most trustworthy outcome.

An analysis of happiness needs to include exploration of the concept of a 'meaningful life'. Meaningful can be considered the answer to questions like: to what does my life amount to? Is this life I am living a relevant one? To whom?

Who cares about me? And why? Freedom to make one's own choices, a sense of autonomy, connectivity, love, feeling productive and not being alone or bored are all elements that contribute to a sense of leading a meaningful life. It is important to consider 'happiness' and 'meaningful' as two different concepts with an overlap which was first defined by Aristotle.

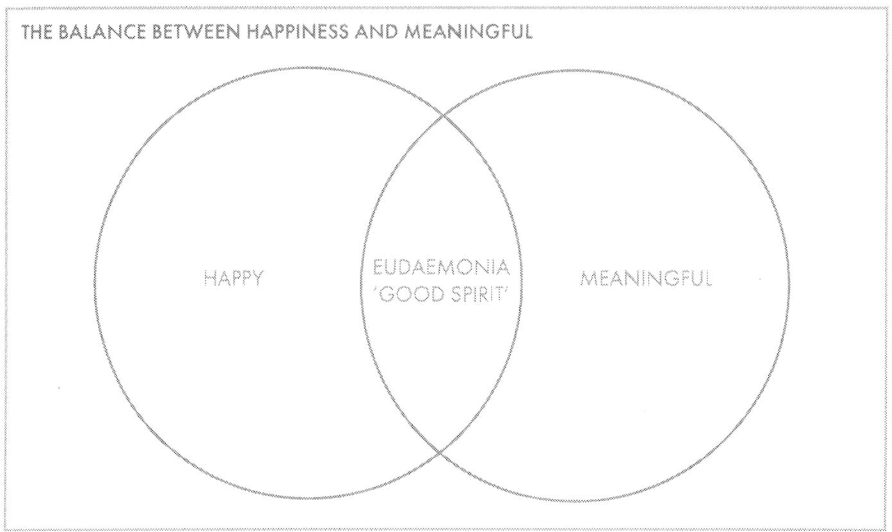

Source: Flex or Fail 2019

People who lead happy, but not necessarily meaningful lives, have generally satisfied all their basic needs: they are healthy, have enough money, and feel good for most of the time.[2] People who live meaningful lives may have none of the above. Another way to put it: happy people live in the present, whereas those with meaningful lives know where they are coming from and where they are going by making plans for the future and setting ambitious goals. Happy but meaningless lives are more about taking and receiving, whereas meaningful lives are about giving and sharing. Parents might appreciate a form of meaning from their children, but not necessarily happiness. Stress, challenges and struggles cause a more unhappy life, but it might simultaneously add more meaning to it.

This might sound controversial, but upon taking a second look it can make more sense. Meaning involves striving for ambitious goals, often at the cost of more immediate pleasures, such as spending time with friends or loved ones. Meaning is also more about freedom and expressing the self rather than satisfying the self, which is one of the central goals that is often pursued in search of happiness. Another important factor is freedom, or autonomy, which is defined as having multiple options to pick from in order to lead a good life (positive freedom) and the absence of coercion that would prevent someone from choosing among those options (negative freedom). It is important to consider that there can be much discomfort in performing activities that lead to a meaningful life. Meaningfulness is therefore more about exploring possibilities and thinking bigger and extends its scope beyond the immediate needs of today's world.

DEMYSTIFYING HAPPINESS

Social critics often express their concerns when observing the state of mankind, such as 'the younger generation is crippled by depression', 'there is a loneliness epidemic' and 'mental disorders are on the rise'. However, research is showing that this is not necessarily the case. Let us demystify some of the newspaper headlines to illustrate that the reality is not as negative as many would let us believe:

Myth 1: It is all getting worse

There is no hard evidence that previous generations were happier than the current ones, although many sources would have us believe this is the case. As a matter of fact, the evidence points the other way: people from all countries are happier now than they were in the past. The World Values Survey, held in 150 countries, stated in 2016 that 86% of the people surveyed are 'rather happy' or 'very happy'.[3]

The graph below shows that satisfaction with life is higher in countries that are relatively wealthier. The general conclusion that many people draw is that citizens will feel happier if their country is growing economically. However, since the scale is logarithmic, one should realize that it takes more dollars to make rich people happier than it takes to make poor people happier.

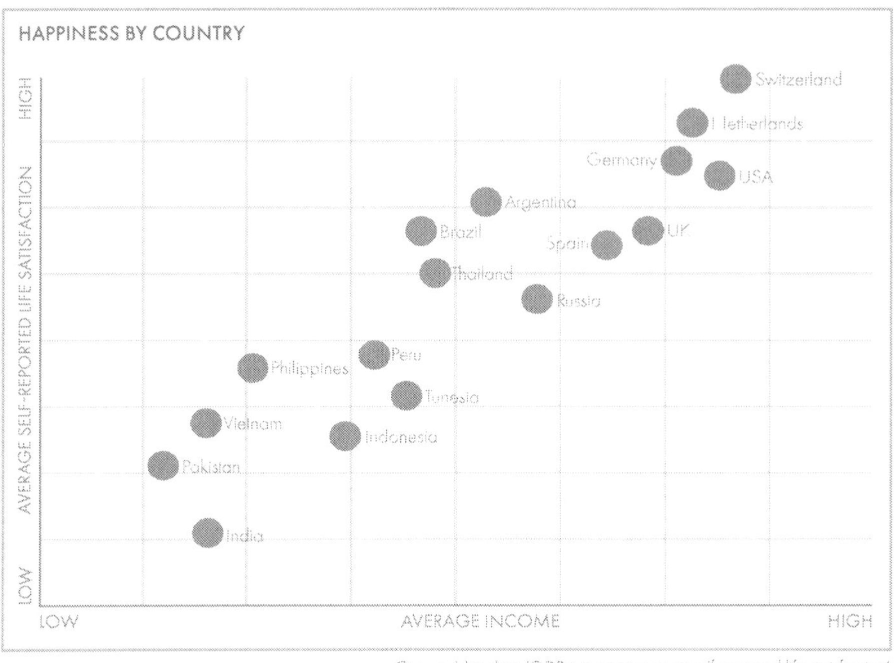

Our world in data 'GDP per capita versus self-reported life satisfaction', 2016

Myth 2: Happiness is a fixed value throughout life

There is no proof that people are born with a fixed level of happiness which remains more or less stable throughout life. Happiness can be affected by adversity, such as the loss of a loved one, and people are simply not always able to bounce back from negative experiences. Likewise, positive events in someone's life can increase their overall level of happiness for a prolonged period.

Older people are usually a little happier since they have overcome and gone past many of the problems of a complex life. People in their early twenties experience a dip in their level of happiness, which is primarily caused by their growing awareness of the challenges ahead and the growing distance between their protected life as a child and adolescent and the beginning of their true independence. Economically good times, with low unemployment and inflation, impact the feeling of happiness positively, while the opposite occurs in an economic down turn.

Myth 3: Migrants are not happy

Happiness of immigrants depends predominantly on the general quality of life they have in the country where they migrated to. Happiness can change, and does change, according to the quality of the society in which people live. An immigrant's happiness, similar to a local person's happiness, depends on a range of features of the social fabric, extending far beyond the higher incomes traditionally thought to inspire and reward migration. Countries with a balanced set of social and institutional support systems deliver happier people.

Myth 4: People are happier in small towns

The Chinese phenomenon where workers move from the countryside to the big cities is sometimes called the greatest mass migration in history. Overall these people feel better and more comfortable with their new lives, although the happiness levels of of city-bound migrants falls slightly below the urban averages of the workers who are already established in their new region.[4]

So what do all these myths and their counter proofs tell us? Let us take a look at independent workers to illustrate the importance of considering meaningfulness and happiness with respect to the working environment and its developments.

Independent workers are forced to re-invent themselves. This starts off with prioritising what is important in their life right now, by making up the balance between monetary goods and non-financial elements of value. One might say that part of growing up is about redefining one's core and its corresponding values. Albus Dumbledore, one of J.K. Rowling's most famous characters, said: "It is our choices [...], that show what we truly are, far more than our abilities". It is very likely that people will have to define their new identities several times throughout a lifetime.

To illustrate the above, we quote from a blog post by Carina:

> *"My career started eons ago! Far too long ago to mention. It has morphed over the years from a clinical to a commercial role, and finally now merges both in a way that I could never have envisaged when I left university. It has skipped across countries and continents, each bringing new lessons and altered perspectives.*
>
> *The biggest leap of faith in myself came later in my career. Jumping from a good position in an interesting company to going back to university to study for a Master's degree might be labelled as a "mid-life crisis" but it turned out to be a saviour. I was fortunate that being out of employment for a year wouldn't matter to my lifestyle.*
>
> *That year of studying served to redefine myself and my professional interests. I met some amazing people that I would never have crossed paths with. Thereafter, a short stint in a large company confirmed everything I disliked about the corporate world, and I joined a small consultancy that I later became partner of. We work virtually, which would not suit everyone, but certainly suits me. Virtual working allows us to transcend geographic divides, cultural barriers and to dream beyond the confines of the rigid office structure.*
>
> *This journey has been exciting and exhilarating, and a way of working that I strongly recommend. However, this recommendation comes with a caution: Virtual workers need to have discipline, a passion for what they do (that overrides the passion for sleeping late, playing TV games etc) and a vision. Turn your work into a passion!!!"*

https://blog.flexorfail.org

This and other interviews show the importance to revisit one's values, or what is most important in life. Previous generations may have valued a job at a large company which offers lifetime employment and decent pay, but if personal growth and exploration is worth more, the leap described above is worth it. Besides the fact that the days of lifetime employment are over, current generations might get claustrophobic in such a situation.

Much of what people spent is going towards status related items. For example, does one really need several expensive and important looking business outfits? These may have been required in corporate life, but are probably less relevant when one is running an Airbnb. The ability to let go of old habits can provide us with new energy and may reduce costs.

Coming back to re-inventing oneself in light of independent working, we should take a look at a number of things associated with full time employment which no one will miss: stress at work, an autocratic boss, office politics (winning might be fun, but how does it feel to lose?), unhelpful colleagues, commuting time, lack of resources, out of date software & systems, ugly buildings, lack of fresh air and unhealthy habits (another birthday cake on the kitchen counter...).

Considering the fact that one does not have to face this when becoming an independent worker makes it seem almost utopian. But there are also disadvantages to not work for one specific organisation. Most people we interviewed mention they miss certain colleagues. Perhaps the toughest one to tackle is losing one's status. Once workers are not associated with any of the big employer brands, are people still as willing to answer their phone calls? Would their personal brand be strong enough to overcome this issue?

BLUE ZONE

Apart from the skills and network that is required to lead a more stable life as an independent worker, it is also important to consider the concept of health. One can assume that health itself is key to wellbeing (mental, physical and social). What can be done to positively influence one's health? What is the reality of old age? Does it always comes with chronic illness, dementia, care requirements, loneliness and loss of autonomy? Or are there choices in the area of eating, drinking, exercise that can have a huge impact 10 years down the road? To answer these questions, we explore the Blue Zone Theory that focuses on diet, exercise, daily rituals (routine), kinship, beliefs and community.

Blue Zones[5] are regions of the world where people live much longer, healthier and arguably happier, than average. Buettner identified five geographic areas where people live statistically the longest: Okinawa (Japan); Sardinia (Italy); Nicoya (Costa Rica); Icaria (Greece) and those that live among the Seventh-day Adventists in Loma Linda, California.

The people inhabiting Blue Zones share common lifestyle characteristics that contribute to their longevity. The people of Okinawa, Sardinia, and Loma Linda share a number of characteristics, which Buettner translates into a list of lessons:

- Moderate, regular physical activity
- Life purpose
- Stress reduction
- Moderate caloric intake
- Plant-based diet (the majority of food consumed is derived from plants)
- Moderate alcohol intake (preferably wine)
- Engagement in spirituality or religion
- Engagement in family life

ment in social life (people of all ages are socially active
eir communities)

workers need to treat their well being with as much respect as their
are many decisions which can be taken today which will have a
act on one's future health. Questions that should be considered are
ealthy years one can expect and how many expensive, care-intensive
head. The difference between 'being happy' and 'living a meaningful
ficant. The interviews have made it clear that becoming independent
ving behind colleagues, but at the same time new doors open and new
wait around the corner. The trick is to make sure one's health and well
eives the attention it needs, in order to enjoy the pleasures of life.

Dr. Richard E.A. More
BM MBA DA DCH DRCOG Dip IMC RCS(Ed)
Operations Director

T. 01935 881630
M. 07787 123912
richard.more@avanaula.com

Avanaula Systems Ltd.
The Vineyard
Little Norton
Norton-Sub-Hamdon
Somerset, TA14 6TE

HOW MUCH IS ENOUGH?

Subject:
There is a number for how much money you need

Key Message
1. That number is lower than you think once you identify your costs
2. Learning from the Stoics

WHAT AMOUNT OF MONEY DO PEOPLE NEED PER YEAR TO BE HAPPY?

This would probably be the point in the book where you expect to see a hard number. It could even be the case that you picked up the book and flipped straight to this point to find some answers. The hard answer is that research shows people in the US need about $75,000 per year (in 2016 purchasing power terms) to reach an optimum level of happiness.[1] This doesn't sound like a lot? You're not alone in thinking that; it is a surprise to many to learn that more money will not give you a proportional extra amount of happiness.

Now think about it another way, there are sources which say that if you can bring your cost of living down to about $35,000 per year and you desire to stop working altogether at the age of 35, you need to have about $400,000 in savings to make it through the rest of your life.[2]

This statement might make this book sound somewhat elitist if you do not earn $75,000 per year. If you are now in your early twenties, without a secure prospect of landing a fixed job with a guaranteed salary, these numbers might seem out of reach. However, to stay true to the optimistic nature of this book, we would say that the best way to get close to these numbers is by selecting an education that provides a practical skill as well as a broad perspective on the international job market. This foundational platform, together with the opportunities to earn from different sources supported by new technology, can set people of on an independent worker course.

ABOUT THE OPTIMUM LEVEL OF HAPPINESS

To expand a bit more on the concept of the ultimate amount of happiness linked to money, let us do a little thought experiment. Think of the following three people who are living in Singapore: Jasmine is a 30-year-old single who works in an

NGO and makes $34,000 per year. Her friend from college, Aisha, takes home $114,000 from a local insurance company, and Evelyne, her neighbour around the same age, makes $192,000 as an investment banker. Who would you think would be the happiest?

You might expect that, obviously, Evelyne would be the happiest of the three, since she earns the most compared to her peers. However, the psychologists involved in this particular field of study find that the one who is making the most money is probably no happier than the one in the middle of the three. They are both earning an income above $107,000, which is the point at which more money (in East Asia) does not yield more happiness. The technical term for this cutoff is the income "satiation point." Following research, the conclusion would be that both top earning people would report slightly higher happiness scores as compared with Jasmine.

The study, based upon data from Gallup's World Poll, which involves over one million people from around the world, finds that, in general, people with higher incomes are indeed happier. The interesting part of it is that there is a level at which happiness no longer increases with more money, an amount that varies by region.[3]

The chart below illustrates this phenomenon of the satiation point for different areas of the world. The incomes are converted to US dollars and adjusted for variations in spending power across countries to make comparisons easier.

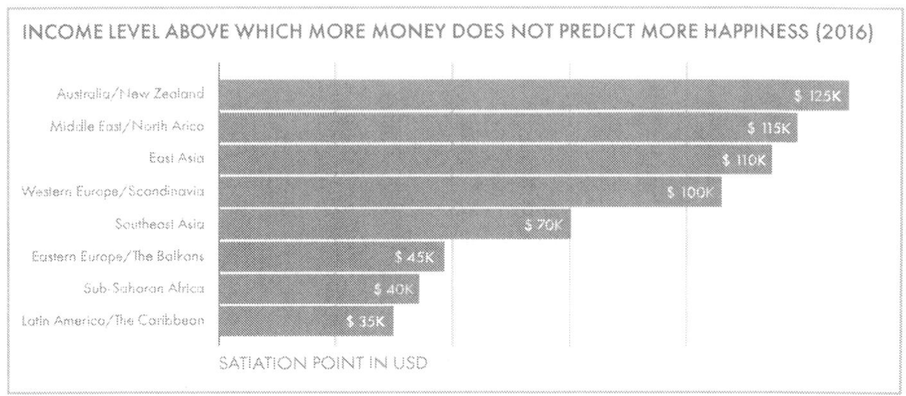

Source: Clifton J.'The happiest and unhappiest countries in the world', Gallup, 20 March 2017

In 2010, the Nobel prize-winning duo of economist Angus Deaton and psychologist Daniel Kahneman, defined the satiation point for US households was at about $75,000.

As stated in their report:

> *"More money does not necessarily buy more happiness, but less money is associated with emotional pain. Perhaps $75,000 is a threshold beyond which further increases in income no longer improve individuals' ability to do what matters most to their emotional well-being, such as spending time with people they like, avoiding pain and disease, and enjoying leisure. It also is likely that when income rises beyond this value, the increased ability to purchase positive experiences is balanced, on average, by some negative effects. What the data suggest is that above a certain level of stable income, individuals' emotional well-being is constrained by other factors in their temperament and life circumstances."*[4]

Further studies explain why rich people do not always have better lives and are not necessarily happier above a certain amount of money.[5] More money impairs people's ability to saviour life's everyday little pleasures, like a walk in the sun or tasting a chocolate. Having access to the best things in life all the time may actually undercut people's ability to reap enjoyment from life's small pleasures.

Now, let's assume you are reasonably happy, but would like a little more freedom and autonomy. How much money would you need to be somewhat independent?

This is where Mr. Money Moustache comes into play, a humorous movement started by Canadian Pete Adeney, who retired in 2005 at the age of 30. Pete and his ex-wife worked in software engineering and had an income of approximately $67,000 per year, per person, over the course of their careers. They lived frugally and invested the majority of their pay during their working years. At the time of their retirement, they had amassed approximately $600,000 in investments in addition to a mortgage-free house valued at about $200,000.

Pete advocates the 4% rule through his blog, which states that, with a balanced investment portfolio, a retiree can withdraw 4% of his or her portfolio's initial value each year, adjusted upward for inflation each year thereafter, with a low probability of ever running out of money.

He only spends a small percentage of his annual salary and consistently invests the remainder, primarily in stock market index funds. The take-home message of his blog posts are about how middle-class individuals can and should spend less money, own less and share more in order to increase their financial independence and happiness as well as a creating a smaller CO2 footprint.

Clearly, this way of living works for him. Is he a one-of-a-kind person? Or are there examples in history which have shown us similar success stories? Let us go back to one of the earliest lessons we can find from Athens, Greece.

The Stoics were founded by Zeno of Citium in Athens in the early 3rd century BC and spread later to Rome and beyond. The core of the philosophy states: "To have a good and meaningful life, one needs to stop chasing an ever increasing list of desires, because it leaves a person no more satisfied at the end compared to how he or she was at the beginning." The Stoics, which is the name of this group of philosophers and their followers, focussed instead on appreciating the things they already had (owned, shared or experienced) and developed techniques, such as visualisation, to help people eliminate a number of anxieties.

There is somewhat of a revival of this concept, or a realisation that we are not approaching life in the right way. Management experts have re-explored the Stoics and their theories by conducting research on the habits of highly effective people.[6] The concept of the 'circle of influence' aims to eliminate anxiety about the present and the future state of the world by separating one's worries into things that can be influenced, and things that can't be controlled.

Worrying about one's health, which is something that many people do, can be reframed by trying to live a healthy life in order to prevent avoidable illnesses. Stoics actually enjoy experimenting with hardship and endurance to challenge the body. A contemporary Stoic might take up sports, like running, in order to experience prolonged periods of exercise that add some contrast, without adding much cost, to a usually comfortable life. By broadening one's comfort zone and being more open to the experience of cold, fatigue and pain, one is ultimately able to reduce such fears, or at least for a while. This is of course not only the case for sports. There are many other ways to slightly decrease the comfort, such as adapting food habits, or not buying a new smartphone every other year, in order to start appreciate other, more important things. By experimenting with voluntary discomfort, people can learn to appreciate more of their day-to-day lives, and become content with less. Living in a simpler and more wholesome way may lead to a more fulfilling and less costly life.

A typical Stoic would be a hard-working person who enjoys the discipline of serious effort, in both work and play. Rich social interactions are high on the priority lists of

Stoics, since they observe that humans are extremely social creatures who benefit from being part of a group. This would tie in directly to the life of independent workers, since part of their safety net and business contacts come from the network and community in which they operate. They also experience 'discomfort' from time to time as a consequence of their uncertain working lifestyle which makes successes such as securing new work or bearing fruits from prudent investments, even more fulfilling.

When dealing with injustice and insults, Stoics would advise to use rationality rather than anger. During work, one constantly has to deal with feedback, both positive and negative. Although negative feedback is never pleasant to receive, the way in which the message is conveyed is of crucial importance, and the Stoics acknowledge this and have a very clear view on the matter, regardless of the situation. If the feedback is true yet unpleasant, both in content and form, the receiver has an opportunity to improve and move on. If the feedback is not true, one should feel sorry for the one who gave the feedback initially and use the opportunity to live a better life. The reason life will be better is that it is now fueled by the conviction that one does not want to end up like the bitter person who made the insult.

Stoics attempt to let reason triumph over emotions and the human condition. By accepting and understanding the inherent evolutionary driving forces (instead of battling against them) people can make choices which support living a happy and meaningful life or seeking a higher level of understanding of the world around us.

To link stoicism back to materialism can act as an eye-opener. The desire to 'have more' could be seen as part of people's original programming; not a character flaw but a 'software bug'. So no need to get angry with yourself for an excessive streak, but to see it as a mere reminder of the human condition. People naturally tend to want 'more' (food, drinks, partners, money, houses, status, security and power), but being aware that one has a choice in these situations, may lead to a more balanced and affordable lifestyle.

This inevitably brings us back to the question: how much is enough? And once we have figured that out, could a new form of wealth distribution as a consequence of the answer perhaps lead us towards a whole new system of work and pay?

When trying to look for answers, we were greatly inspired during one of the major design events held in the Netherlands. The Dutch Design Week features 260 graduates of the Design Academy in Eindhoven who showcase their work. In 2018 graduate student Martina Huynh exhibited an installation called Basic Income Cafe, which explores the relation between work, pay and jobs. She uses coffee as a metaphor for the flow of money[7]

The opening question in her video work revolves around the approach of her generation to work and how this is vastly different from her parent's generations in terms of status, income and security. By asking the "Why do you work?" question, she explores if we work to get money with which we can buy coffee in the Basic Income Cafe or if we could work and get the things we need right away, like coffee.

The last question would almost immediately lead to the thought of eliminating a money system, a concept that she further explores in her art. This is an installation where coffee takes the place of money. Everybody in this fictitious world of the installation has the right to one cup of coffee without doing anything - so one cup of coffee represents your basic income. You need the coffee because it gives you the energy to perform the jobs, or look for other jobs, that are available in the Basic Income Cafe.

If you want more coffee, you can execute tasks in the Cafe such as the 'grinding' where you process the beans to powder. This gives you the right to another cup of coffee. Or, to be more precise, to another half of a cup of coffee. The other half goes into the 'commons', which is the inventory of coffee from which other people get their daily shot of caffeine. This would be the equivalent of a 50% income tax rate. Here's the drawback of the experiment: what if no one would like extra coffee? Who would fill the 'commons'?

With her intriguing fictional world, she raises questions about the efficiency and competence of our current system, while at the same time rattling the chains of

Source: Graphic by Flex or Fail 2019

politicians who advocate the creation of more jobs. Do we need more jobs? Or does a country just needs to provide its people with the security of a basic income, instead of jobs?

In this perspective, the recent article[8] in the Financial Times by Lawrence Summers is interesting. It explores the feasibility of providing all workers in the US with a job. This idea, supported by progressive politicians, is (according to the article) driven by studies that show that those without jobs are much more likely to be dissatisfied with their lives, to become addicted to alcohol or drugs, and to be abusive within their family than those people working on low wages they consider inadequate. The conclusion of Mr Summers is that the plan is not affordable and he suggests that a combination of wage subsidies, targeted government spending, support for workers with dependants, and increased training and job-matching programmes represents a more viable strategy for meeting demand for guaranteed employment.

The remaining question is how people would behave if the stress of securing an income was replaced by the security of knowing there is enough for a person to live on, with the encouragement to find the job they like? This question could trigger a new economic development phase, if there were enough solutions to some of the more basic problems at hand; enough money to start the transition and a business model which allows a country to support its citizens.

Perhaps technology could assist us in growing towards such a world. Imagine, we would 'pay' the robots to do valuable and export-worthy work, and the robots generate enough income for the country or region. Meanwhile we humans, would perform more creative tasks such as developing new experiences and services which could lead to future income streams. Arts would become an richer source from which we could imagine different ways to live, work and play while taking care of each other. How would we value contributions from other people in terms of humour, entertainment, innovation and education? Would that give them access to a cup of coffee?

Chapter 19 looks at people who defined their 'how-much-is-enough' number and brought cost in line with their new life style. As you will see from their stories, it is possible to live the dream.

19

PEOPLE WHO LIVE THE DREAM

Subject:
There are people who are doing what they want to do, i.e. living the dream

Key Message
1. Taking control of your working life
2. Enthusiasm, creativity and passion are muscles which need to be trained

"Living the dream" basically means "living the type of life you want to live without any regrets. Achieving all your goals. Enjoying the fruits of your labour". There are people who have become the master of their own destiny. Through our interviews and social media interaction we have found they share a number of characteristics.

Most have dealt effectively with ego, status and the urge to 'keep up with the Jones'. Where did they find the confidence, focus and reset buttons required to set out as an independent worker? Who told them about hitting the 'ctrl - alt - delete' button to reset the expectations as they went independent?

Let's take a look at a number of examples of people who contributed to our blog on blog.flexorfail.org and see what lessons can be distilled from their experience. These are people whose transition from employment to independent working has been made possible through their use of enabling technologies and the use of platforms, in combination with their skillset and progressive mindset.

The first example is Eleanore, a 52 year-old woman living in Germany's well-developed Ruhr Gebiet. As her education during her teenage years had stressed the importance of working hard and being able to take care of yourself financially, she became a highly successful finance professional. She eventually made €100,000 a year. However, she quit after 25 years, as she felt she wanted to do different things, albeit for a lower salary. She is not bothered by the reduced income and has acquired enough self knowledge to understand what is of value to her, beyond the money. A very inspiring example. But how does she manage the decrease in income?

Her personal business model is based on the knowledge that she needs roughly €2,500 per month to live, work and play. During her career she saved €200,000 and made another €200,000 in real estate investments. She knows she will get €45,000 per year through her pension fund from the age of 65 which is enough for her to live on. In order to bridge the 13 years between 52 and 65, she knows she needs roughly €200,000. She has this amount of money in the bank, but prefers to invest part of this in a rental on AirBnB. As she does not have children, she is not interested in leaving capital behind. She does want to take care of her older father and has created a living space which can serve as a 'sheltered living' accommodation for him, or herself, as and when needed.

Clearly, she has thought this through very well, taking into account possible setbacks and still having enough money left to enjoy a comfortable life. Eleanore has undertaken careful planning to mitigate the risk of a reduced income following the resignation of her job. In order to make her new life a success, she defined three important elements which helped her with the transition from being employed to being an independent worker:

- Revisit your belief system
- Reduce your costs and obligations
- Define what is important to you and what makes you happy

Her personal business model is dynamic and constantly updated to reflect new priorities based on changing conditions. It gives her autonomy and flexibility, two important aspects that can greatly improve mental health and general quality of life. Eleanore clearly understood the key points of making such a transition and how to do so successfully.

We also received a blog post from Roland, who moved from Northern Europe to Mexico at the age of 34 and has been making a living in the sun for the last 20 years. He addresses you - the reader - directly, to give you an idea about his experience.

> *"Back in high school I had several conversations with two friends about wanting to explore the world, rather than just staying in our home country. We looked forward to waking up with sunshine and live in paradise. Every year we would travel to a tropical country, also to see how it would be to*

be there for the long term. We did research on legislation around owning property, the possibilities to work as a foreigner, how to get residency permits, while not forgetting about more basic things like the quality of the food, security, the people and culture. After finishing Japanese studies and Philosophy at university it was time to work so that I could save enough to realize the dream. I worked in IT for ten years, which was most of the time great fun and enough to save the required amount of money.

However, it has to be said I had my ups and downs financially. At one point I had saved € 100,000, but I soon lost about €50,000 on the stock exchange. These fluctuations and uncertainties pushed me to ask myself how much would be enough. I decided not to focus too much on the amount of money but instead put more emphasis on the amount of energy. My theory was that to be able to build up a completely new life, one has to have enough energy (no matter how much money). This proved to be true and a valuable lesson before taking the leap.

In 2006, at the age of 34 I gave a goodbye party and went to Mexico. The first five years I created a business from scratch and ran two bar/restaurants on the beach. I still own one that I rent out but for the last 7 years I have dedicated my life to construction. When you do not depend on others or the amount of money on your bank account, stress is greatly reduced. And you might wonder what my friends from high school did? One lives in Malibu Beach in the U.S.A. as music is his passion and that place offers him the possibility to work with the greatest artists. The other one is a pilot and visits us once in a while."

We love both these examples. These are real people who defined their 'dreams' in a thoughtful and responsible manner. So which dreams do you allow yourself? What holds you back? When is the optimum moment to execute some of your plans taking into account the energy required to build the dream? You might think the two examples only apply to young people. Let's take a look at someone in her eighties who is an independent worker with an agile mindset.

"I am 83 and provide independent psychological assessment of the learning needs of children and young adults. My work is about helping teachers and parents understand why their children or pupils are not performing as well as they could, and recommending appropriate actions to help them to learn better and improve their exam results. I receive referrals from former colleagues and my professional network. Age does not affect my line of work so much, and the experience of having seen so many pupils helps. I think this is greatly satisfying, but am planning to retire at 85 and pass the requests on to other educational psychologists, despite the demand for my services still being there.

In this case, it probably is not about the money. This lady feels she has a worthwhile skill and enjoys to contribute to the learning success of future generations. She is part of a network and probably experiences great job satisfaction. Her line of work allows for careful selection of the number of sessions she can do per day, depending on her energy levels and schedule."

We can make a next step of what it would mean to leave one's current job and to start up a portfolio life. Here's a story by Eva from Greece.

"When I was 18 years I started working while studying at the same time, as I felt I would be better off being financially independent. For many years I worked hard, seven days a week. I pursued an MBA at ALBA school. Since graduation I have worked in eight different companies and I'm only 39 years old as I write these lines! I have also worked in four different countries, so changing companies was inevitable. Despite all difficulties associated with so much change, I must admit I enjoyed the ride and I still do.

And now there is another change knocking on my door: the FLEX change. I have decided I don't want to spend the next 20 years of my business life in an office, obliged to abide by the rules set forth by people or corporate cultures that will try to put at rest or suppress my growth potential, creativity, willingness to make a difference, readiness to help. An inward looking corporate culture that doesn't embrace change and growth, can harm people. Everybody knows this. So I'm becoming independent by establishing my consulting company.

I will basically continue doing the same thing I did the past 12 years (marketing and product management); the difference now is that I can arrange my schedule (and my office) as I please. This, nevertheless, doesn't necessarily mean I will be working less. I hope this change will give me the opportunity to share with more people the experiences I gained while working in eight companies and four countries. I have a lot to give and I know there are people out there that are willing to take a risk and learn - people that I couldn't possibly reach, if I wasn't flex."

In this case, Eva has made a clear choice to make a decisive leap. She has gained international experience and a high level of relevant, professionals skills. Most importantly, she has the energy and passion to strike out on her own and she is, using her own words, flex.

Assume you have made the change and you are now living in a place of your choice with multiple income streams coming in. In other words, you have achieved your objectives. What could threaten your model? Who is coming after you to get your money? How can you protect your health and well being? Who is there to help out and how do you seek out services that you need to support you? Where do like minded people live? These are questions for all people who are making the change to independent working. We are curious how this feels when you are in your twenties, so Eileen, a 27 year-old digital artist from Birmingham, provided an insightful commentary.

"I finished art school at 22, and launched my own studio. During my studies, I held several part time jobs to pay my way through the academy. After school it all went quite quickly. I've been lucky since my work has been bought by several European Museums and I've had a number of exhibitions at galleries. I love the freedom and autonomy of being a small entrepreneur and being independent, but at the same time the pressure to both create and sell is highly demanding.

There is a team of five people depending on me and their salaries need to be paid every month. Sometimes I'd love to have the security to know that my own salary would be a guaranteed amount of let's say 25,000 pounds per year, but that is a luxury I don't have. My husband is also an independent worker who takes on projects for clients. The situation is becoming increasingly complex because his skills are also needed in my art studio. He would sometimes ask me: "should I take this 4,500 UKP gig or should I work on your art?" That makes me acutely aware of the opportunity cost and the real money that in a way should be priced into my work.

It's all about managing the highs and the lows and balancing various priorities. So far, I have not taken other jobs, as I'm fully focused on making the studio a success. For the moment, I would not want it any other way and if the successes keep on coming as they have done so far, I can think about things like pension, savings and, who knows, even investing a little."

These real world examples are coming from people that have made the switch. We have changed the names in order to protect privacy, but these examples demonstrate the careful planning that went into becoming an independent worker.

The remarkable high level of energy, and these people's enthusiasm to take responsibility for their own lives is inspiring. All of these people showed a curious mind and a willingness to keep on learning in order to stay relevant in a changing world. It was clear that they had supporting networks in place and had invested in education. In these cases, being independent worked well. Our next chapter will take you to a different place, a future which might come about if we fail to manage the application of technology correctly.

20

WORK DYSTOPIA

Subject:
What 'bad' could be like for workers

Key Message

1. Global megatrends have the potential to massively change society
2. Megatrends combined with technology could make it better or worse

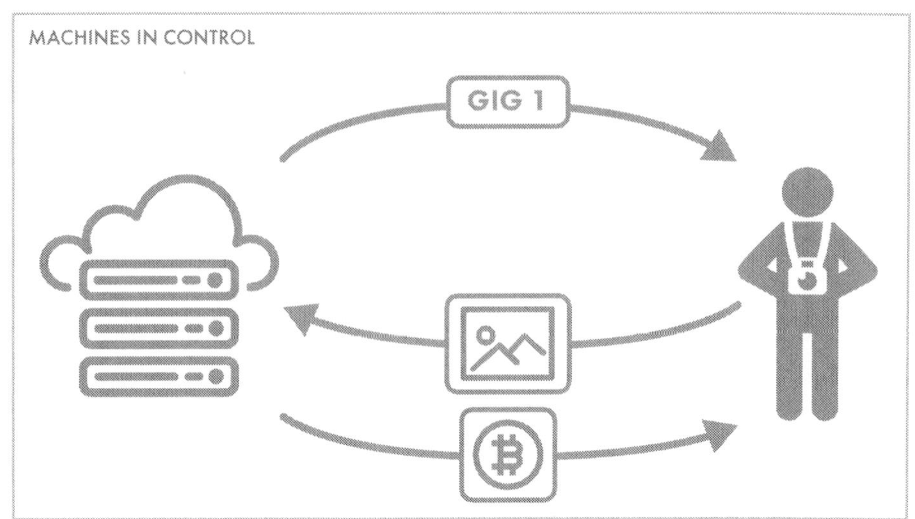

Source: Flex or Fail 2019

A voice from the internet: Frank, a 'dayjob worker'

> *"I'm 28 years old. After I dropped out of college, I found a job in a distribution warehouse. I needed the money to pay off debts. The job was low level and poorly paid. I increasingly worked alongside machines, including robots. I was made redundant and then worked in a call centre, but again, the job became automated and I was out of work.*
>
> *Lately, I have not been feeling quite myself. I now live on the internet, which is to say, I am living in my parents' basement. I do dayjobs that come through a variety of channels; text message, social media, email, and anonymous robot dialers.*
>
> *They are always executed on the blockchain and they pay out in cryptocurrency. I personally use an aggregator app that is able to login to all of my accounts and scrape them for contracts. You cannot ask for a dayjob, the dayjob has to come to you. The more dayjobs you complete, the more frequently they will come.*
>
> *Most of the actual jobs are simple. For one job, I was told to go to a certain address and take a photograph of a building at a particular time. Regardless of who the buyers of these services are, they must have some particular goals, although I don't know what they are.*
>
> *Something is happening in our society at a vast scale. Whether it is being controlled by machines or not, I don't know. I need the money to live, but I have no certainty of the future or who is in charge any more. It's a frightening situation.*

What is the risk that your job will be replaced by a machine? What income streams can you rely on if your main job disappears? Will your skills still be relevant so that you can continue working, even after the age of 60, and maybe for another 20 years after that? Are you worried about your children's future?

This chapter looks at the future, how megatrends will reshape the working environment and what risks individuals and organisations face. This is more complex than simply stating that jobs are being lost to automation, but encompasses the transition process for workers to adjust to the 'new normal' as well as the impact on income levels. Getting this right can drive productivity and economic growth. Getting it wrong could lead to a dystopian future that goes far beyond work and pay. Future risks may lead to fragmentation of society and could disrupt social cohesion, affecting individuals' well-being on a large scale.

MEGATRENDS THAT WILL RESHAPE ECONOMIES BY 2030

"Prediction is very difficult, especially if it's about the future" said Nobel prize winner Nils Bohr. But even if the future will remain uncertain, forecasting is important for planning as these megatrends are already happening and have a major effect on people, work and pay.

A report by KPMG describes key megatrends that will reshape economies by 2030.[1] These megatrends can be clustered in and around three groups: those affecting the global economy, those affecting the physical environment and those that affect individuals.
Global economic megatrends are based on assumptions about economic power shifts, public debt levels and economic interconnectedness. A key megatrend that they predict will be that by 2030, economic power will shift from developed to developing countries, who will by then account for 57% of the global GDP. Facilitated by new technologies and a dynamic consumer-driven workforce, these

economies will grow faster than developed economies, which will be hampered by a shrinking labour market and rising social costs.

Another prediction is that the growth in net public debt in developed economies will increase to 98% of GDP by 2035. This rise is mainly a consequence of the ageing population which escalate healthcare and pension costs. Although the predictions for international trade are more positive, with an estimated growth of 5% annually, there are also risks around rising trade barriers that may in turn undermine this economic growth.

Physical environment megatrends are focused on climate change, resource stress and urbanisation. Climate change is familiar to us all and a commitment was made at the 2015 Paris Agreement to limit global warming to less than 2 degrees Celsius, with a target of net zero emissions by 2050. This would cost between $70-100bn per year till 2050, of which 75% would be paid for by developed economies. A recent report by the IPCC recommends temperature is reduced further to 1.5 degrees Celsius, but even before this recommendation was made, the C02 reduction targets were already missed.[2] Consequences of continuing global warming include extreme weather effects, rising sea levels, displacement of people and threats to industries such as agriculture.

Stress on natural resources also comes from needs of an expanding population, rising expectations from economic growth and an ongoing demand for water, agricultural output and energy resources. With a global population of 8.3bn by 2030, a 50% increase of food production and 40% increase of demand for water supply is predicted. This will lead to an increased competition for natural resources, potentially leading to environmental destruction, species extinction and potential for conflict.

By 2030, some 60% of the world's population will live in cities. The number of megacities, which are defined as cities that have a population of more than 10 million people, will rise to 37 by 2025. Although this may stimulate economic and social development, it will also have significant consequences for the demand on infrastructure, including housing, water and energy. Currently, one billion people live in urban slums, a figure that is predicted to double by 2030.[3]

The final set of megatrends are those that affect individuals, including demographics and technology. Of all the megatrends we describe, demographics can be seen as the 'iceberg,' as the effect is only partially visible at present, but the submerged bulk will increasingly appear with shocking effect on the future of developed economies.

Japan is the 'bellwether' economy that can illustrate this iceberg effect, with the highest average life expectancy in the world at 84 and over 28% of its population over 65. This compares to 21% in Germany, 15% in the US and only 6% in India. Japan already suffers from an acute labour shortage which will only increase over time, as well as a spiralling growth in welfare costs that contribute to a public debt of 250% of GDP.

Higher life expectancy and falling birth rates are observed across most developing economies. Increasing longevity is clearly a 'good news' story for most of us, but its downside includes higher costs of public healthcare and pension provision, which exacerbates the feeling of unfairness amongst younger generations. Additionally, as the proportion of people of working age drops, the labour force starts to shrink, unless people work for longer. This adversely affects economic output and productivity.

The final megatrend we address is the empowerment of individuals, especially women, through improving education and better access to technology. The expansion of the 'middle class', defined as individuals earning between $10-100 per day, is already transforming developing economies. KPMG predicts that 60% of the global population will be defined as 'middle class' by 2030, with 80% of the global middle class residing in developing regions.

In tandem with individual empowerment, access to new technologies is 'powering up' the new middle classes. 75% of the world's population already has access to a mobile phone and half the population will have access to the internet by 2030.[4] This will dramatically improve their ability to communicate, innovate and engage in entrepreneurial activities, further stimulating economic growth in developing economies.

THE IMPACT ON WORK AND PAY

What do these megatrends mean for work and pay? Firstly, there is the 'march of technology', which lies at the base of all the factors mentioned above. In the future, machines and platforms will not only enable humans to develop novel solutions, but multiple technologies working together in a coordinated way will enable transformational change in many industry sectors. These advances will not just be technical, but increasingly implemented and applied to everyday work tasks, thus affecting more and more existing jobs.

Jobs that require data processing or repetitive physical tasks are at a higher risk of being replaced by automated processes. Roles that require a higher degree of creativity, empathy and judgement are at lower risk. A McKinsey report shows that across international economies, up to 20% of work activities could be displaced by 2030.[5] The transformation of industry sectors such as retail, transport and manufacturing will affect large numbers of existing workers. However, the report also shows that demand for labour will rise across various sectors in the developed world, especially professional, managerial and care related roles.

The picture of technology displacement of existing jobs is thus not as black and white as we might think. Some jobs will vanish, but new ones will emerge. Crucial to this trend is the provision of support for workers who are in transition between roles. The evidence shows that if displaced workers do not make the transition within one year, they are at a greater risk of a prolonged period of unemployment. Managing the transition of workers is therefore the key priority for policymakers, organisations and individuals.

Advances in automation and technology can and will produce significant productivity gains and, overall, support economic growth. However, a recent report showed that in the UK, around one third of the value of wages and earnings has the potential to be automated, with low wage jobs more at risk than high wage.[6] In essence, there could be a significant transfer of national income from wages to profit. This would affect whole regions, whose workers are deployed in lower paid occupations, further exacerbating income inequality. Without careful management, overall society may become richer, but the losers become poorer.

MANAGING RISK AND WHAT IF IT GOES WRONG

If you think the account above represents a science fiction view of the future and you can hear yourself say "let's get back to business as usual", think again. Consider Frank, the individual whose working life is described at the beginning of this chapter. Frank is a troubled person who feels isolated, not in control and obviously fearful about his future.

Frank is not on his own. Artificial intelligence is already leading to increasing surveillance in the workplace with apps and sensors that monitor individuals performance and track movement to an increasingly sophisticated degree. Organisations can now monitor and evaluate individuals in real time obtaining objective evidence, and as a consequence, can quickly replace poor performers. So, what's wrong with a manager who simply wants to improve efficiency? Technically nothing, but increasing intrusion into the personal workspace may also have an adverse effect on workers' attitude and their mental health.

Increasing application of monitoring technology in the workplace bears its risks, primarily with dehumanising processes. Chatbots replace human interaction, apps monitor browsing history and emails in offices and algorithms select job candidates. Furthermore, if such algorithms are not programmed carefully, they can perpetuate systematic bias and prejudice. As technology becomes more pervasive, individuals and their experience at work may become more stressful.

Frank, our voice from the internet, also shows signs of depersonalisation and derealisation. He comes across as lacking emotion and living in a world that is strange, detached and unreal. Clearly, there may be other things going on in his life but it is a fair assumption that his role as a lone dayjob worker is at least partly contributing to his mental health issues.

The relationship between job loss and mental health issues is well described in literature.[7] Loss of income, self-esteem and social contact all contribute to this association, as we have pointed out before. The impact on people's mental health includes depression, alcohol abuse and suicide. Job loss and independent working can also lead to social isolation and loneliness. Prolonged social isolation particularly affects younger and older people. In Japan, recent statistics show that more than half a million people in Japan stay at home for at least six months, making almost no contact with the outside world.[8]

There are wider risks resulting from the emerging megatrends. For example, climate change is having an effect on migration particularly in sub Saharan Africa, South Asia and Latin America. A World Bank report estimates some 143 million people worldwide as 'climate migrants' at risk from crop failure, rising sea levels and water shortages. Many of these people will become cross border migrants escaping from poverty and oppression if their home economies fail to diversify and create more climate-resistant jobs. A consequence of this will be mass migration to countries that offer jobs and a more stable future. This may be welcome in some developed economies, whose working population is shrinking due to demographic changes. However, if this is not managed, a rapid influx of migrants may stoke nationalism and the perception from the host population that their jobs are at risk from lower paid migrants.

We have outlined in this chapter how forecast megatrends are likely to unfold and impact labour markets at the individual and country level. A dystopian future for workers can be prevented by effective planning and reforms by policy makers and organisations. Individuals can take actions that mitigate risks to ensure their future participation in meaningful work. The biggest risk of all is inertia and lack of timely actions. The speed of change is greater than most organisations and individuals currently believe. The race is on to see if necessary change can be made in time to save Frank, and others like him, in the future.

21

FLEX TO SUCCEED

Subject:
Individuals need to take ownership of their jobs and income

Key Message
1. We outline a 5-step approach for people to undertake this
2. Cities are the center of opportunity for professional development and social interaction

"Automation is certainly affecting the demand for labour. Take Amazon for example, it is hiring 20,000 fewer workers in the US in the winter of 2018 than the previous year, which analysts attribute to greater use of robots in its fulfilment centres"[1]

In Chapter 20 we described key megatrends that will shape economies. However, in spite of all the predictions and economic modelling, we simply can't be certain about the speed of automation and how it will affect specific job roles across different economies.

What we do know for certain is that change is coming. Therefore, what can people do to prepare themselves to adapt to the coming changes of automation in their workplaces? Individuals who rely on their government or their firms to take the lead may be putting their future at risk. In this chapter we will argue the case for being proactive and the type of actions individuals can take to survive and thrive in a world of increasing automation. We suggest five key steps (visualised in the graphic), which are:

1. Evaluate how much your job and industry sector are at risk
2. Identify options for transition
3. Planning for new ways of working
4. Embrace life-long development
5. Engage with your neighbourhood and urban community

TAKE CONTROL NOW

Source: Flex or Fail 2019

1. EVALUATE HOW MUCH YOUR JOB AND INDUSTRY SECTOR ARE AT RISK

All industry sectors will be affected by automation to some extent. This means that all jobs are potentially at risk of being altered, but not necessarily, being replaced. But how much might your industry sector or job role be affected in the future? McKinsey estimate that between 400-800 million workers globally will be displaced by automation and will need to find new jobs by 2030.[2] Of these, up to 375 million people may need to switch to new occupational categories and learn new skills.

Tasks that will be particularly affected include predictable physical tasks such as food preparation and material handling, as well as office support roles such as procurement, payroll and administration. In all, up to one third of the workforce in the US and Germany, and a half in Japan, may need to find new occupations by 2030, since they all occupy jobs in these different sectors.

A report from PwC, that analysed 20,000 jobs in 29 countries, outlines which industry sectors are at the highest risk of being replaced by automation. Sectors such as transport, with development of autonomous driverless vehicles, and

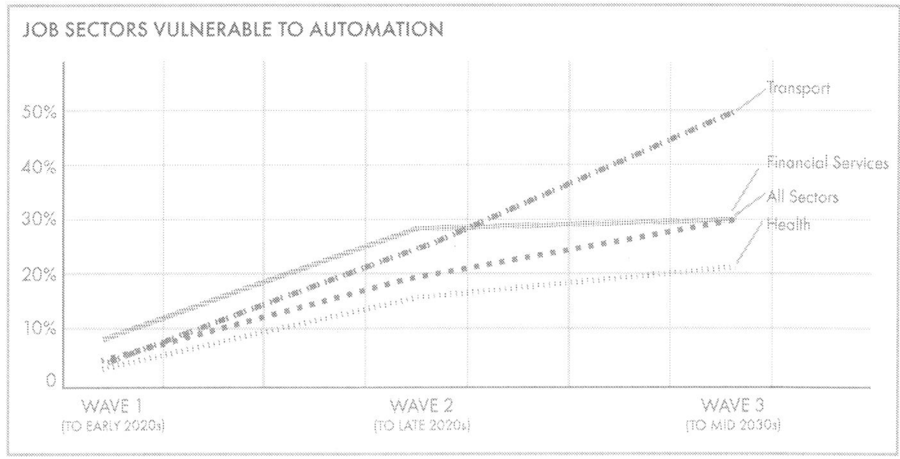

Source: PwC estimates based on OECD PIAAC Data (median values for 29 countries)

financial services, where algorithms will replace human analysis, will be particularly affected. Healthcare and education workers are at lower risk of impact from automation, because social skills and human interaction are intrinsic to their role. However, even in these sectors, new technologies will be increasingly deployed. Robots are already used in Japan and Europe to assist in activities that support reminiscence therapy for older people with dementia, such as playing memory games. Workers in these sectors will need to adapt their roles to work alongside a range of new technologies.

People in the workforce, as well as those about to enter the workforce, should carefully consider the potential impact of automation on their industry sector and their job role. They should regularly research and 'scan the horizon' with regard to technology developments in their profession, role and organisation, and constantly evaluate the level of risk to them, well before their job may be put 'at risk'.

2. IDENTIFY OPTIONS FOR TRANSITION

What can people do if they think their job is at risk, or when they have been informed that their job is being made redundant as a consequence of automation? The good news is that many new jobs will be created in parallel to those lost to automation. The challenge for individuals is their approach to the transition to new roles or working lifestyles, or adaptation of their current job in order to integrate with new technologies.

Clearly, the possibilities of such a transition and the opportunities for the creation of new jobs, is highly dependent on the nature of the sector and the specific role individuals are engaged with. For example, the advent of robotic surgery has been transformative in some areas of surgical treatment, such as prostate cancer. Surgeons would have to undertake specialist training to use such machines safely and effectively, but so far there have been no reports of significant job losses as a consequence. Nevertheless, automation will affect many workers, and jobs such as warehouse operatives as described at the start of this chapter, are already disappearing.

Companies and organisations have a pivotal role to play in terms of workforce planning as a consequence of adopting new technologies. Many forward-thinking organisations are already investing in education and skills training to re-equip their workforces. Other skilled workers will play a key part in enabling their organisations to adopt new technologies, whether that is as part of technical project teams or wider change management initiatives.

Individuals will therefore need to make choices as to how they plan their future careers, be it within their chosen job or specialty, or in pursuit of a different line of work or model of income creation, as described in previous chapters. All these choices have risks and will require planning and development of new skills.

3. PLANNING FOR NEW WAYS OF WORKING

Irrespective as to whether you are starting work, are mid-career or pre-retirement, managing risk for individuals starts with planning. Ask yourself some of the following questions: how much is your job at risk from automation? What would be the time frame in which this might happen? What alternative work would you want to do if this risk was high? Do you have the skills for this and if not, how could you acquire them? Who would you reach-out to for help in making this transition?

Planning can be as structured or not as individuals desire, but engaging in a planning process is in itself part of the individual's journey of transition. Thinking, researching, analysing and discussing these concerns are an essential part of the mix that helps to form a vision and a 'call to action'. This is as much driven by individual passion, a sense of identity and clarity of a vision, as it can be a 'tick a box' checklist needed to be fully prepared for the next job interview. As such, this could also be broadly seen as a step towards a personal transformation as we have seen from people's personal accounts in chapters 16 and 19. At the end of this process, individuals may be left with a set of choices, at which point it is invaluable to have wise counsel from trusted family, friends and colleagues that can provide constructive challenge to help make wise decisions.

We know that an individual's willingness to accept and embark on a programme of change is highly dependent on their mindset and personality. The psychologist Carol Dweck demonstrated how people can be dramatically influenced by how they think about their talents and abilities.[3] In her research, she divided people into two groups: people with a fixed mindset who believe that abilities are fixed, and people with a growth mindset who believe that abilities can be developed. Her research showed that the former group is less likely to adapt to change without clinging on to fixed values and beliefs. People with a growth mindset were more likely to flourish as a result of change. Dweck showed that, with the right mindset, individuals can motivate others and transform their own lives to become more successful.

There is not a single blueprint for an individual's transition planning. The speed and impact of the changes we describe are of a magnitude that the solution can only be discovered by individuals themselves, through imagining how future risks and opportunities may impact them, and what actions they will need to take to shape their own agenda. Clearly, the scope and direction of an individual's future is shaped by their skills, experience and preferences, but in order to become 'forward looking' they will need to nuance this around new activities and combinations that are innovative and create value.

As part of planning, we have previously highlighted the need for diversification of both income streams, and work activities to create resilience and maximise opportunity. For most people, assuring an income would be the 'number one' issue when looking at risk management and building resilience. However, many families in the US and other developed economies experience a high level of income and consumption cost volatility from month to month. This can ultimately create financial risk as well as anxiety and stress. Recent research from the US showed that the average American has a personal debt of $38,000, ex-mortgage.[4] Another survey showed that 44% of people claimed that low income was the primary reason for being in debt. After mortgage debts, the most common reason for debt was student loans and credit card debt (both around 20% of total). 29% of the sample said that they thought they would never get out of debt, with one in three wanting to get rid of credit card debt as their highest priority.[5]

Clearly mortgage and student debt could be viewed as being 'good debt', but credit card debt, with high rates of interest, is seen as 'bad debt' and something to minimise if at all possible. The need to review and manage costs, generate extra income, increase levels of savings and budget carefully are important measures needed to mitigate risk, and should be included in transition planning.

4. EMBRACE LIFE-LONG DEVELOPMENT

Improving skills levels increases productivity and economic growth. The historic convention of the three stages to people's lives, education, work and retirement, is rapidly changing. As the nature of work evolves, so should education, learning and development in order to run in parallel throughout people's lives to ensure that their skills in the workplace remain aligned to changing demands.

Education needs to start at an early age, as the importance of a child's early years lays the foundation for the future. Research has demonstrated that the human brain develops at the highest pace between birth and three years old, which makes that period the most important one for learning new things. The intake of information at this age is critical to healthy and effective neurological development.[6] Governments and parents need to ensure this 'golden window' of development is properly addressed as a foundation for the future.

Does the current education system deliver outputs needed for a changing work environment? With the demand for maths, science and technology skills, such as coding and programming, predicted to rise by 55% by 2030, many countries lag behind in their capacity to deliver necessary skills that address this level of demand.[7] Clearly, many aspects of traditional education are behind the curve with what will be needed.

The demand for skills is changing from manual and routine cognitive labour to non-routine analytic and interactive labour that requires greater social skills. A report from the World Bank outlines in more detail the skills required, including: accessing and analysing information, problem solving, learning and communication skills, self-management and social skills.[8]

Business leaders are increasingly questioning the relevance of a university degree in terms of providing graduates with meaningful skills. Business schools also recognise the need for radical change in both the design of business education, and how they engage with their alumni more effectively throughout their working lives. Some experts believe that the scope of this type of education needs expansion, with a greater emphasis on subjects such as philosophy, drama, storytelling and psychology that forge creative thinking and help stimulate innovation.[9]

Beyond conventional education institutions, how will individuals get access to skills development at the scale that is needed and what systems need to be in place to make this work? There is an explosion of innovation in this sector that is recasting how conventional education systems will evolve in the future. Some examples include:[10]

- **Microlearning**: this approach uses videos, apps and other tools, presented through online channels, to deliver specific information with very short courses (from a few minutes to 20 minutes) that may include a quiz at the end that provides credentials for continuing professional education
- **Massive online open courses (MOOC) and open sources of education:** provide online access to high quality content from leading academic centres such as Stanford University (whose first course in 2011 on Introduction to AI reached 160,000 students)
- **Virtual conferences:** which provide online access to wider audiences at lower cost and higher convenience
- **Gamification:** whereby the concept of online gaming is applied to the learning environment by utilising team dynamics, competition, collaboration, joint learning while at the same time promoting greater engagement
- **Social learning:** a concept whereby people learn from one another, via observation, imitation, and modelling. It encompasses attention, memory, and motivation and has more recently been applied to support learning through social media, for example through 'personal learning networks'

These examples of new ways of accessing skills and learning materials will grow and evolve as demand for such services intensifies. New forms of recognised credentials are being created that will expand alongside traditional degrees and diplomas. These will become a more recognised currency and include structured citations and testimonials from work undertaken to a high standard. Flexibility is key, with an ever-expanding group of people accessing skills development at different entry points beyond traditional education pathways.

There are 500 million video plays per day on YouTube in the category instructional videos, meaning more people are helping themselves to fix things or solve issues independently than ever before.[11] Can you imagine the workplace without online video tutorials as a way to quickly find out how something needs to be done, paraphrased by some as "YouTube to the Rescue"? It has become an accepted practice in the work environment where 'knowing-everything-by-heart' is replaced with the 'ability to find, learn and use'. At home, a similar development is taking place. When was the last time you read a printed instruction manual for a device or service? This would probably have been a while ago as the internet is a better and faster source for enquiries to fix the constantly beeping oven or to reset the error code on the washing machine. Online learning is on the rise, and it's going up fast.

Who is benefiting from free online education? In other words, who is getting smarter here? Coursera, Khan Academy, Udemy and Skillshare serve an audience of educated, curious people. Interestingly enough, those that follow courses on the platforms are often already qualified people with college and/or university degrees. Apparently, this group has embraced the concept of lifelong learning through informal ways of keeping up to speed with the job market.

With such a plethora of new approaches to learning emerging, the traditional system of education and skills credentials will need to be broadened to include people who have not gone through traditional channels for qualifications, as well as those seeking quicker routes to upskilling.

Organisations will also need to become more proactive in upskilling their workforce (be they employed or temporary). A broad range of possibilities for additional training and education that is more flexible than the traditional education, will open new doors for both employers and employees to adapt to changes without having to lose their workforce. By mapping future job roles to the competencies that will be needed, firms will be able to identify gaps and plan more accurately to support learning requirements. Governments will need to reform their education policies to ensure that both younger and older people are able to adapt and transition to new working conditions.

For individuals, life-long development will happen in a multitude of ways: some of it will be formal through more traditional education, but most will be less formal, through interaction with people and selective self-development effort. Our core message in this chapter: 'flex to succeed', will partly depend on individual's ability to continuously identify what skills they believe they will need beyond the horizon. This will enable them to adopt a more entrepreneurial approach to be able to navigate through the world of work and take necessary steps for proactive development.

5. ENGAGE WITH YOUR NEIGHBOURHOOD AND URBAN COMMUNITY

Gaining access to work opportunities is rapidly transitioning to digital platforms as a first port of call, as these can more easily match people and their skills with available jobs. Building a compelling personal online profile is key to the successful marketing of an individual's skills and experience. This may be augmented by citations from previous employers and clients that add authenticity and personalisation. Becoming part of online professional groups and networks further adds value to individuals in terms of a virtual community that can provide opportunities and ideas.

Both virtual and physical communities are important for social connections and these are especially important for independent workers as a means of both social support and networking. Developing social connections is however not confined to the digital world, and many thinkers believe that local communities, both in cities as well as rural areas, are crucial to sustain society as it becomes more fragmented. Social infrastructure is evolving from more traditional venues where people aggregate, such as places of worship and libraries, to new environments such as collaborative work- and living places like WeWork, Selina and Venn City, as well as neighbourhood café's and bars. Proponents of social infrastructure challenge the dominance of virtual communities and champion that real social connections between people need to be forged and integrated within their local communities.

The rise of the independent worker is in part related to growing urbanisation. The trajectory of growth of independent working in the future is somewhat dependent of whether the city of the future will have design characteristics related to the lifestyle of independent workers.

As a Harvard academic described, 'cities are vehicles for transmitting knowledge and ideas.[12] They facilitate faster innovation, which is what companies active in the knowledge economy are looking for, in order to stay ahead of competition. Cities with top quality universities also attract employers who need a supply of highly qualified talent from an international pool. These two parties in turn can improve the overall quality of the local labour market even further.

Recent developments in various countries and markets show that this effect is increasing. In 2017 Amazon said it would open a second headquarters outside Seattle and the company invited bids from cities for the 50,000 new jobs and $5bn in investment it would bring to the table. In November 2018 Amazon announced it would build not one but two new offices and split them between New York City and Arlington, a suburb of Washington, DC. These innovations are welcomed by the local governments and cities as it provides employment opportunities and can give a boost to the local economy. Other big firms have similar intentions; Google has also announced plans in 2018 to hire more workers in New York City, outside their head office in Silicon Valley.

The decision to bring so many high-paying jobs to successful cities is part of a broader trend. Employers like to be in the places where there is world class talent. Since these jobs are well paid, the prices for housing in these areas go up, making it increasingly expensive for anyone with an average or lower income to live there. The countryside and smaller cities may be at a disadvantage in terms of knowledge development and could face difficulty in attracting talented people as well as employers.

The key message for ambitious, independent workers, especially the young, is that cities are becoming ever more the hub for professional opportunity and social interaction to forge a successful career.

Clearly, as independent workers and people transition to new work roles, they will need to engage with both online and offline channels in order to build their profiles and networks. Social support is vital to sustain individuals through times of uncertainty, to share experience and provide support. Identifying and planning how networks and communities may be engaged and utilised will become a key success factor for workers who want to develop their brand, sustain a more flexible form of working, and lead (more) fulfilling lives.

22

EPILOGUE

By 2030, advances in automation and new technologies will have changed the nature of many work activities, and displaced some groups of workers all together. In total, this is likely to affect some 60% of the workforce. As a consequence, the level of independent workers in developed countries is likely to double. The speed and impact of these changes is as yet, not well recognised by most people or employers.

The picture we have described in this book presents both threats and opportunities, and investigates why the structure of work and pay in the future will be different from the past. We have purposely focussed our narrative around individuals, as they will need to make plans and decisions that can help protect them from the worst effects of a rapidly changing labour market. But we have also outlined that individuals need to consider not just their work, but also their way of living and wellbeing.

The examples we describe in the book have shown how many of these threats can be mitigated by careful planning, support from other people and sheer determination. We also highlight that having professional skills, an open mindset and being based in a city are likely to be advantages.

We have focussed in the book on people who are either dissatisfied with their current work lives, or who see the world changing around them and want to plan for such changes in order to achieve a more fulfilling lifestyle. Drivers of this change include the evolution of the new 'gig economy' and lower barriers to enter, start and grow micro businesses.

We have described in some detail how the various generational groups have different priorities when it comes to work, pay and lifestyle aspirations. These groups will be affected in different ways by future technological disruptors. We have outlined why multiple small income streams are of key importance to independent workers who need to develop resilience and manage risk that will come from a rapidly changing job market.

For organisations, and the people that lead them, an insight into how individuals will be affected is critically important as these are the people who make up their workforce, customer base and indeed stakeholders in society that will increasingly dictate policy. Individuals in most countries also vote for their political representatives and protest in the streets if they are not being listened to. Overall, the wellbeing of individuals matters, and that includes the security and satisfaction that their work provides.

Our message is one of cautious optimism whereby a greater level of autonomy that most independent workers currently describe could be embraced by many more people. This is tempered however by the threat of uncertainty of income, loss of benefits and isolation.

Policy makers need to look deeper into those leading countries and economies which are adopting new strategies to both promote and protect independent workers, and especially how they may be re-skilled and benefit from new forms of lifetime learning. For countries to retain competitive advantage, this area of policy will be high on the list of priorities.

People who have read the book will hopefully consider their own situation in a new light and will seize new opportunities as a result of this. If we have signalled the level of urgency and stimulated a 'call to action' by our readers, the book will have achieved its goals.

FROM THE AUTHORS

Strava is the place where this book started. This sports-platform was a great tool to coordinate plans to write a book together. The ability to see each other's cycling performance proved highly motivating and brought the discipline to combine work and play. For urgent matters, there was always WhatsApp to trigger the next decision. We hardly ever used the phone, but did take the time to organise writers' retreats where cycling and craft beers took center-stage.

What we enjoyed most of all was the synergy between our attitudes and skills. Writing a book together in a well designed, creative process is more fun than doing it alone. As a matter of fact, that would be our recommendation to others: find one or more partners, engage a great support team, commit to a print deadline and stop watching Netflix for 6 months. We would wish you well in such an endeavour.

From here, we are going to continue to write articles about Work & Pay, Urban Tech, Smart Cities, Healthy Ageing, Living in Communities and Competitiveness. We'll be happy to provide strategy consulting on these topics and would be delighted to speak at your events!

Visit our blogs on www.flexorfail.org or drop us an email at info@flexorfail.org and we'll make it happen.

ACKNOWLEDGEMENTS

We would like to thank our editorial team who have worked with us to create the book you are holding now. Julie, representing Generation Z, was our editor from the start. She provided energetic and professional support, right from the early stages of developing the book. Peter, representing the early Millennials, has been the creative producer who designed all visuals and artwork. Without his technical understanding of the publishing process, our workflow would have been much less organised. Dennis, representing the late Millennials, took responsibility for all web development and social media components.

The book was enriched by people writing blog posts on www.flexorfail.org. Martin, Richard, Deborah, John, Eleanore, Eileen, Eva, Carina, Roland and Nancy; we thank all of you for your willingness to share such inspiring stories.

Lesley and Elise were our proofreaders and represented yet another generation and demographic. We have taken your comments to heart and hope you will recognise where your contributions made a difference.

Esther, Maaike and Eva were our Generation X reviewers. Your interest, intelligence and capacity to deal with us during the writing process is much appreciated. We wrote much of this with Generation Z in mind and Felipe, Amanda, Iris and Ruben delivered constructive provocation which made the book more future proof.

A special thank you goes to the team at IMD where Katie, Vincenzo and Maelle coordinated, scheduled and supported our work. Haley, Aïcha, Mike and Lucy boosted the visibility on all media, including social, of this book and we are very grateful for your enthusiasm and professionalism.

There are many other people who contributed to the book and influenced our thinking. To them we express our sincerest appreciation.

GLOSSARY

Adjustment Costs

The costs associated with making any changes. For example, the costs of buying machines to replace manual work

Agile team

A self-organising, cross disciplinary team of diverse people who are collectively responsible for all the work that is required to produce and validate outputs according to the project's specification

Baby Boomers

Demographic description of the generation born between 1946 and 1964

Blockchain

A digitised, decentralised public ledger of transactions that allows participants to keep track of transactions without the need for central recordkeeping

BREEAM

Building Research Establishment Environmental Assessment Method is the world's longest established method of assessing, rating, and certifying the sustainability of buildings.

Comparative advantage

An economic term that refers to an economy's ability to produce goods and services at a lower opportunity cost than that of trade partners

Defined benefits pension

A defined benefits pension plan is a type of pension plan in which an employer/ sponsor promises a specified pension payment, lump-sum (or combination thereof) on retirement that is predetermined by a formula based on the employee's earnings history, tenure of service and age

Demographics

Statistical data relating to a population and particular groups within it, often used to segment populations for analytical purposes such as marketing

Dependency ratio

The age population ratio between people typically not in the labour force and those typically in the labour force, which is used to measure the pressure on the productive population

Distributed Autonomous Organisation (DAO)

A Distributed Autonomous Organisation, sometimes called a Decentralised Autonomous Organisation, is an organisation represented by rules encoded as a computer program on the blockchain that is transparent, controlled by shareholders and not influenced by a central government

Employee turnover

The rate at which employees leave a company and are replaced by new employees, usually calculated on an annual basis

Entrepreneur

A person who sets up a business or businesses, taking on (financial risk) in the hope of a return (profit, or non-profit)

Fintech

Products and companies that employ newly developed digital and online technologies in the banking and financial services industries

Flex worker

Work practice that allows employees a certain degree of freedom in deciding how their work will be done and how they'll coordinate their schedules with those of other employees. The employer may set certain limits such as minimum and maximum number of hours of work per day and the core time period during which employees must be available

Formal organisation

A group that is structured in such a way so that it achieves its goals efficiently on behalf of its stakeholders

Fourth industrial revolution

The fourth major industrial era, since the first industrial revolution in the 18th century, which is characterised by a fusion of technologies including: physical, digital and biological

Freelance

A person who works on a contract basis for different organisations rather than working as an employee for a single company

GDP (gross domestic product)

GDP measures the output produced by factors of production located in the domestic economy regardless of who owns these factors

Generation X

Demographic description of the generation born between 1965 and 1980

Generation Y also known as Millennials

Demographic description of the generation born between 1981 and 1996. This generation reached young adulthood in the early 21st century

Generation Z

Demographic description of the generation born in 1996 or later

Gig economy

A labour market characterised by the prevalence of short term contracts or freelance work as opposed to permanent jobs. Sometimes also called task economy

Green New Deal (GND)

A proposed economic stimulus program in the United States that aims to address both economic inequality and climate change

Income inequality

The extent to which income is distributed in an uneven manner among the population

Independent Worker

Independent workers are self-employed people who provide services for an organisation under a contract. They do not have an employment contract

Initial public offering (IPO)

The first sale of stock issued by a company to retail or institutional investors on a stock market

Knowledge based economy

An economy that has a greater dependence on knowledge, information and high skills levels, and the increasing need for ready access to all of these by the business and public sectors

Labourtech

Technology that supports independent workers to improve their work and pay conditions individually and collectively

Megacity

A city with a population of more than 10 million inhabitants

Millennials also known as Generation Y

Demographic description of the generation born between 1981 and 1996. This generation reached young adulthood in the early 21st century

National debt

The total amount owed by a government to its creditors

NEETS

People not in employment, education or training

Non Governmental Organisation

A non-profit organisation that operates independently of any government, typically one whose purpose is to address a social or political issue

OECD

The Organisation for Economic Co-operation and Development is an intergovernmental economic organisation with 34 member countries, founded in 1961 to stimulate economic progress and world trade

Personal entrepreneurs

A descriptive term that applies to independent workers who take on a degree of risk similar to that of an entrepreneur, but with the objective of achieving personal financial goals rather than developing a more traditional form of business enterprise

Platform economy

Economic and social activity that is facilitated by online platforms which include transaction and matchmaking services

Portfolio career

The fact of having several professional activities at the same time rather than a single full time job

Portfolio theory

A framework for assembling a portfolio of assets such that the expected return is maximised for a given level of risk

Personal net disposable income

The amount of money that households have available for spending and saving after income taxes have been accounted for

Productivity

Productivity in economics measures output per unit of input, such as labour, capital or any other resource

Return on equity

A measure of the profitability of a business in relation to the equity

Semi private network

A connection within a specified network which has restrictions established to promote a secure environment

Sharing economy

An economic system in which assets or services are shared between private individuals, either for free or for a fee, typically by means of the Internet and online platforms

Social enterprise

An organisation that applies commercial strategies to maximise improvements in financial, social and environmental well-being

Social entrepreneur

A form of entrepreneurship that focuses on the development of innovative solutions to societal challenges such as social, environmental and cultural issues rather than the pursuit of profit

Urban Tech

A sector of innovation that encompasses products that make cities and urban spaces more connected, livable, and efficient

Zero hours contract

An employment contract that does not guarantee a minimum number of hours

APPENDIX A - IMD WORLD COMPETITIVENESS RANKING

The IMD World Competitiveness Yearbook (WCY) has measured the degree of competitiveness of countries since 1989. In the 2018 report, 250 indicators were used to measure competitiveness, which were grouped into four factors: economic performance, government efficiency, business efficiency, and infrastructure. The IMD World Competitiveness Ranking analyses 63 economies covered by the WCY. The rankings are calculated on the basis of the 50 ranked criteria, of which 30 are 'hard data' and 20 'survey data' points.

The 2018 report reinforces a critical trait of the competitiveness landscape, that countries will undertake different paths toward competitiveness transformation. The top five economies remain the same countries as last year, but they have either shifted up or down in the ranking, based on their indicator scores in the four groups.

The United States returned to the top of the ranking, claiming the number one spot as the most competitive economy in the world, which was driven by its strength in economic performance and infrastructure factors. Second in the ranking was Hong Kong that took a different approach by using government efficiency and business efficiency. Singapore maintained the third spot, not moving up or down from 2017, ranking high in the government efficiency and economic performance categories. The Netherlands moves up one spot to the fourth best economy, swapping with Switzerland which moves down to 5th.

The bottom five economies altered their performance that specifically affected countries that have experienced economic and political distress in the last few years. Mongolia ranked 62nd and Venezuela 63rd which remains in the last position. Brazil comes in at 60th with slight improvements but not enough to get out of the bottom five economies. Brazil's improvement is the first since 2010, due to a positive shift in real GDP and employment.

A CLOSER LOOK AT THE UNITED STATES

The United States moved up primarily because of two categories: economic performance and infrastructure. So, let's take a closer look at the sub-factors within those two factors, as well as the other factors:

The economic performance factor is comprised of: domestic economy, international trade, international investment, employment, and prices. The US stayed the same

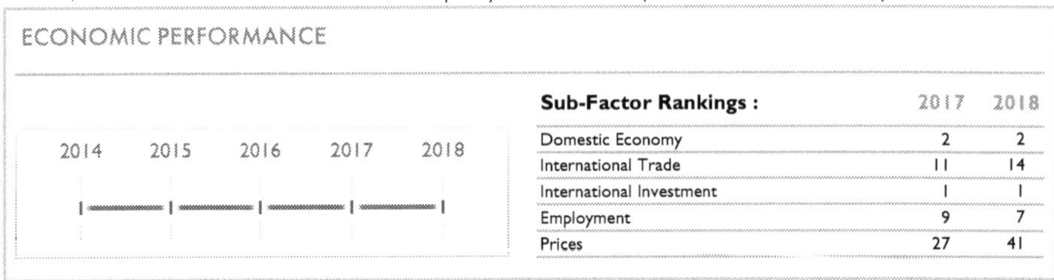

Sub-Factor Rankings :	2017	2018
Domestic Economy	2	2
International Trade	11	14
International Investment	1	1
Employment	9	7
Prices	27	41

Source: IMD World Competitiveness Yearbook 2018

when it came to domestic economy from the year of 2017 to 2018, ranking second overall in the sub-category. The international trade fell from a rank of 11 to 14, but the country remained 1st in international investment from 2017 to 2018, so there was no change. Employment improved moving up from a score of 9 to 7, but prices fell from a score of 27 to 41 which was the biggest transition within the economic performance factor.

The infrastructure factor is composed of: basic infrastructure, technological infrastructure, scientific infrastructure, health and environment, and education. The

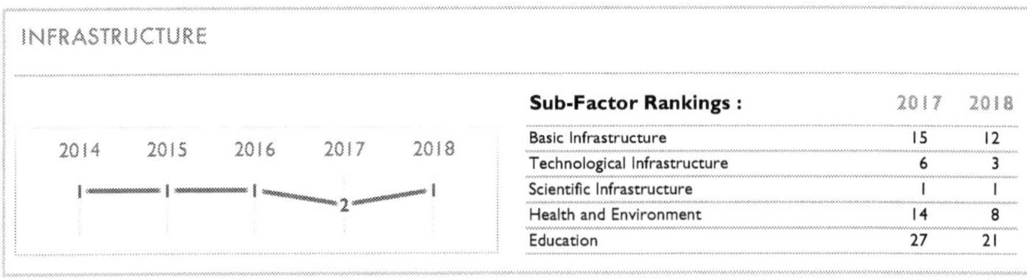

Sub-Factor Rankings :	2017	2018
Basic Infrastructure	15	12
Technological Infrastructure	6	3
Scientific Infrastructure	1	1
Health and Environment	14	8
Education	27	21

Source: IMD World Competitiveness Yearbook 2018

following changes were implemented from 2017 to 2018. The basic infrastructure improved form a score of 15 to 12, technological infrastructure improved from a rank of 6th to 3rd place, while scientific infrastructure has remained number 1 for two years in a row. Health and environment improved from a rank of 14th to 8th, and finally education improved from a rank of 27th to 21th.

The government efficiency factor includes: public finance, tax policy, institutional framework, business legislation, and societal framework. Public finance worsened

GOVERNMENT EFFICIENCY

2014	2015	2016	2017	2018
22	23	25	27	26

Sub-Factor Rankings :	2017	2018
Public Finance	48	51
Tax Policy	31	22
Institutional Framework	24	23
Business Legislation	15	14
Societal Framework	33	34

Source: IMD World Competitiveness Yearbook 2018

from a rank of 48th to 51st, and tax policy improved from 31 to 22. Institutional framework had a slight improvement from 24 to 23, while societal framework fell slightly from 33 to 34.

The business efficiency factor is comprised of: productivity and efficiency, labour market, finance, management practices, and attitudes and values. Productivity and efficiency stayed the same from 2017 to 2018, while the labour market improved

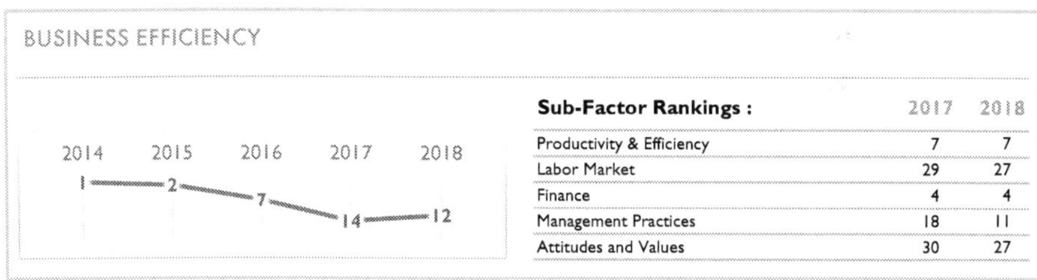

Sub-Factor Rankings :	2017	2018
Productivity & Efficiency	7	7
Labor Market	29	27
Finance	4	4
Management Practices	18	11
Attitudes and Values	30	27

Source: IMD World Competitiveness Yearbook 2018

from 29 to 27. Finance stayed the same with a top score of 4 during both 2017 and 2018. Management practices improved from rising in rank from an 18th to 11th overall, while attitudes and values improved by rising from 30 up to 27.

A CLOSER LOOK AT HONG KONG

Hong Kong moved down one spot and did well in two different factors from the other countries listed in the top five economies. In 2018, the government efficiency and business efficiency factors were the primary drivers of Hong Kong's competitiveness. So, let's take a closer look at the sub-factors within those two factors, as well as the other factors:

The first factor is **government efficiency**: Public finance improved from second place to first place. Tax policy stayed the same at second place both for 2017 and 2018, but institutional framework slipped from a rank of 7th to a rank of 9th.

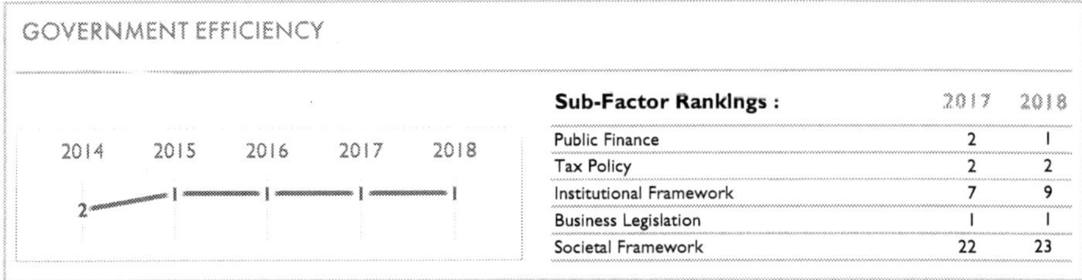

Sub-Factor Rankings :	2017	2018
Public Finance	2	1
Tax Policy	2	2
Institutional Framework	7	9
Business Legislation	1	1
Societal Framework	22	23

Source: IMD World Competitiveness Yearbook 2018

Business legislation remained number 1 for both years, while societal framework got slightly worse moving from 22 to 23.

The second factor where Hong Kong showed great strength was in **business efficiency** where the country stayed in first place in this factor for both years. The

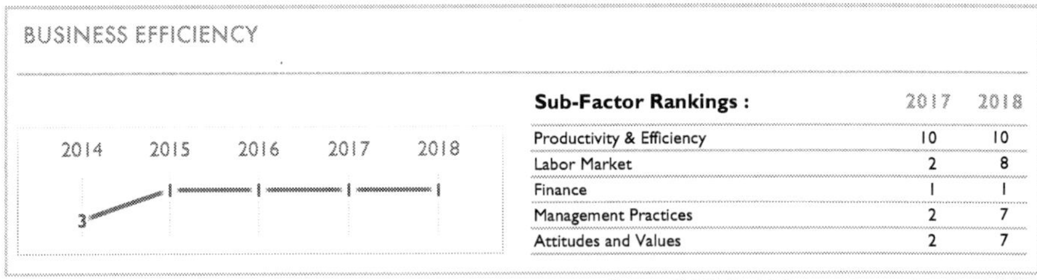

Sub-Factor Rankings :	2017	2018
Productivity & Efficiency	10	10
Labor Market	2	8
Finance	1	1
Management Practices	2	7
Attitudes and Values	2	7

Source: IMD World Competitiveness Yearbook 2018

productivity and efficiency sub-factor remained the same from 2017 to 2018, maintaining a score of 10. The labour market got worse, slipping from second place to 8. Finance stayed at number 1 for both years, while management practices slipped from second place to a rank of 7. Attitudes and also slipped from second place to a rank of 7.

The **economic performance factor** collectively improved from 11 to 9. This factor includes the domestic economy sub-factor, which improved from a score of 26

Sub-Factor Rankings :	2017	2018
Domestic Economy	26	20
International Trade	2	3
International Investment	4	3
Employment	15	12
Prices	62	61

Source: IMD World Competitiveness Yearbook 2018

to 20, while international trade got slightly worse dropping from second place to a score of 3. International investment improved going down from fourth place to third place. Employment improved from a score of 15 to a score of 12, while prices improved from 62 to 61.

The infrastructure factor collectively went down three places from an overall score of 20 in 2017 to 23 in 2018. The basic infrastructure sub-factor improved from a rank of 19 to 6. Technological infrastructure got slightly worse falling from a score

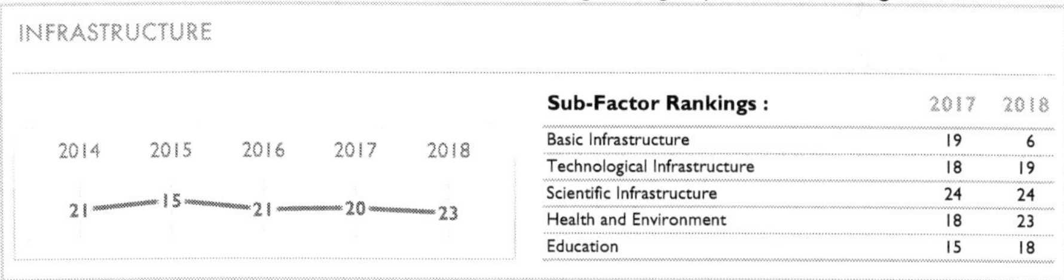

Sub-Factor Rankings :	2017	2018
Basic Infrastructure	19	6
Technological Infrastructure	18	19
Scientific Infrastructure	24	24
Health and Environment	18	23
Education	15	18

Source: IMD World Competitiveness Yearbook 2018

of 18 to a 19. Scientific infrastructure stayed the same at 24 in both 2017 and 2018. Health and environment fell from a rank of 18 to 23. Education also fell from 15 to 18.

A CLOSER LOOK AT SINGAPORE

Singapore remained in the third spot within the top five economies, not moving up or down in 2018. Singapore's path differs from both the United States and Hong-Kong. The factors in which Singapore uses to drive its competitiveness are government efficiency and economic performance.

The government efficiency factor had an overall score of third place. The sub-factor includes public finance which improved from a score of 5 to 3, and tax policy improved from a score of 16 to 13. The sub-factor institutional framework slightly

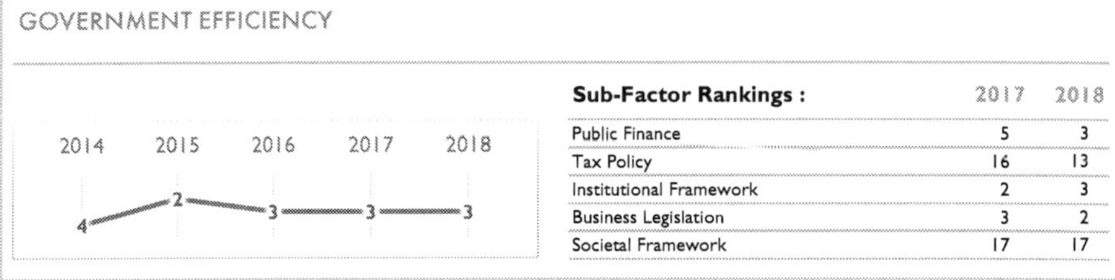

Sub-Factor Rankings :	2017	2018
Public Finance	5	3
Tax Policy	16	13
Institutional Framework	2	3
Business Legislation	3	2
Societal Framework	17	17

Source: IMD World Competitiveness Yearbook 2018

worsened dropping from second place to third place, while business legislation improved from third place to second place. The societal framework sub-category remained the same for both years, receiving a score of 17.

The economic performance factor had an overall score of 7 which went up from 6th place in 2017. Domestic economy improved from a score of 15 to 7, while

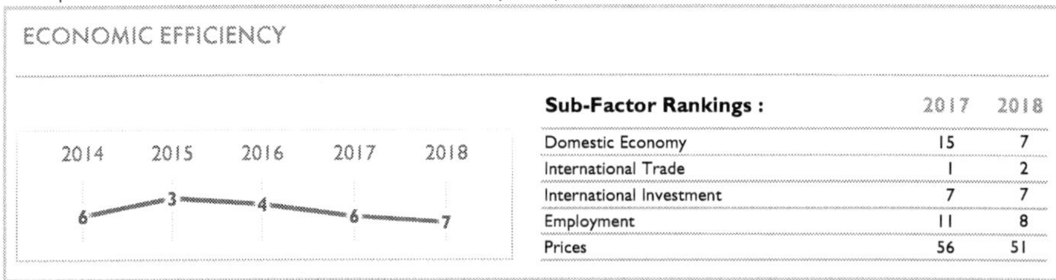

Sub-Factor Rankings :	2017	2018
Domestic Economy	15	7
International Trade	1	2
International Investment	7	7
Employment	11	8
Prices	56	51

Source: IMD World Competitiveness Yearbook 2018

international trade dropped from 1st place to 2nd place. International investment stayed the same at 7 for both years, but employment improved from 11 to 8. The last sub-factor of prices improved from 56 to 5.

The business efficiency factor collectively slipped by one overall score, moving from a rank of 10 to an 11. The sub-factor of productivity and efficiency worsened, moving from a rank of 6 to 15. The labour market improved from 11 to 10, but the finance stayed the same with a rank of 7. Management practices slightly dropped

BUSINESS EFFICIENCY

2014	2015	2016	2017	2018
7	7	5	10	11

Sub-Factor Rankings :	2017	2018
Productivity & Efficiency	6	15
Labor Market	11	10
Finance	7	7
Management Practices	17	18
Attitudes and Values	6	9

Source: IMD World Competitiveness Yearbook 2018

from a rank of 17 to 18, and attitudes and values worsened by moving from 6th place to 9th place.

The infrastructure factor overall went down slightly with an overall score in 2017 of 7 but going up to 8 in 2018. The basic infrastructure sub-factor fell from second place to 7th place. The technological infrastructure dropped from first place to second place, while the scientific structure dropped from 12th place to 17th place. Health and environment remained the same sitting at 25 for both years. Education improved from 5th to second place.

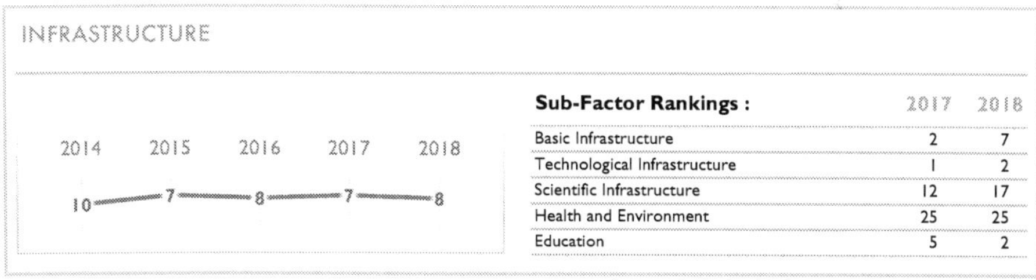

Sub-Factor Rankings :	2017	2018
Basic Infrastructure	2	7
Technological Infrastructure	1	2
Scientific Infrastructure	12	17
Health and Environment	25	25
Education	5	2

Source: IMD World Competitiveness Yearbook 2018

A CLOSER LOOK AT BRAZIL

Some economies are failing with low scores in virtually every factor and sub-factor, but each country has a different reason as to why they have virtually no competitive advantage. Brazil comes in at number 60 out of 63 countries which is one of the worst economies in the world. Let's analyse the factors starting with the worst categories for Brazil, which would be government efficiency and economic performance. The rankings associated with these two factors are almost the complete opposite of the top economies' scores.

The government efficiency factor overall score was 62 and remained the same for two years. The public finance sub-factor score stayed the same at 63 as well as

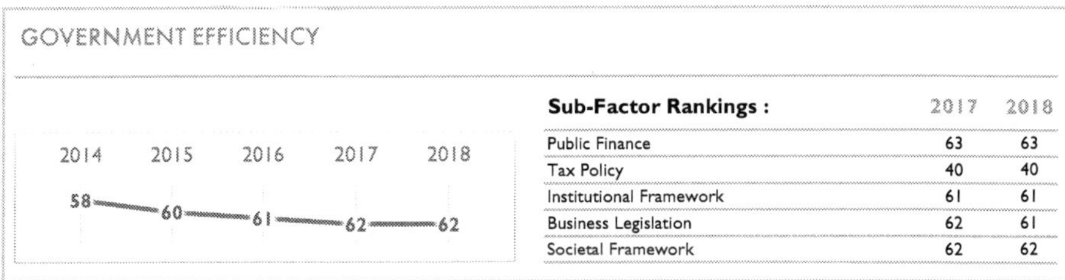

Sub-Factor Rankings :	2017	2018
Public Finance	63	63
Tax Policy	40	40
Institutional Framework	61	61
Business Legislation	62	61
Societal Framework	62	62

Source: IMD World Competitiveness Yearbook 2018

the tax policy score which was 40 for 2017 and 2018. Another two sub-factors that remained stagnant were the institutional framework with a score of 61, and societal framework at 62. Business legislation improved a bit from 62 to 61.

The economic performance factor ranked an overall score of 59 in 2017 but improved to 54 in 2018. The domestic economy improved from 58 to 50 while the

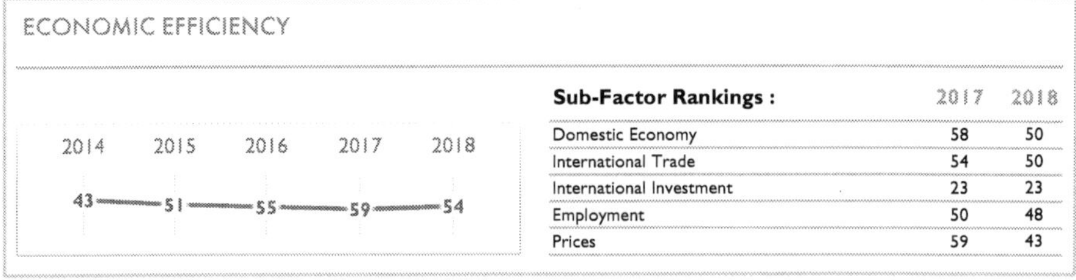

Sub-Factor Rankings :	2017	2018
Domestic Economy	58	50
International Trade	54	50
International Investment	23	23
Employment	50	48
Prices	59	43

Source: IMD World Competitiveness Yearbook 2018

international trade improved from 54 to 50. International investment remained the same staying at 23 for both 2017 and 2018. The employment sub-factor got better as well moving from 50 to 48, while prices improved from 59 to 43.

The business efficiency factor got worse from 2017 moving down from 49 to 50. The sub-factor of productivity and efficiency got slightly better rising up from 60 to

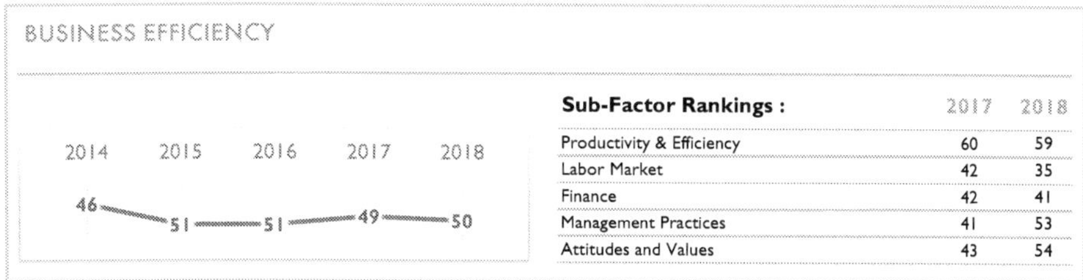

Sub-Factor Rankings :	2017	2018
Productivity & Efficiency	60	59
Labor Market	42	35
Finance	42	41
Management Practices	41	53
Attitudes and Values	43	54

Source: IMD World Competitiveness Yearbook 2018

59, while the labour market improved from 42 to 35. The finance also improved going from 42 to 41 while the management practices got worse from 41 to 53. The last sub-factor attitudes and values worsened with a ranking of 43 to 54.

The infrastructure factor's collective score fell from 51 to 52. The basic infrastructure improved slightly moving from 56 to 55, while the technological infrastructure improved from 51 to 48. The scientific infrastructure remained the same, sitting at 41,

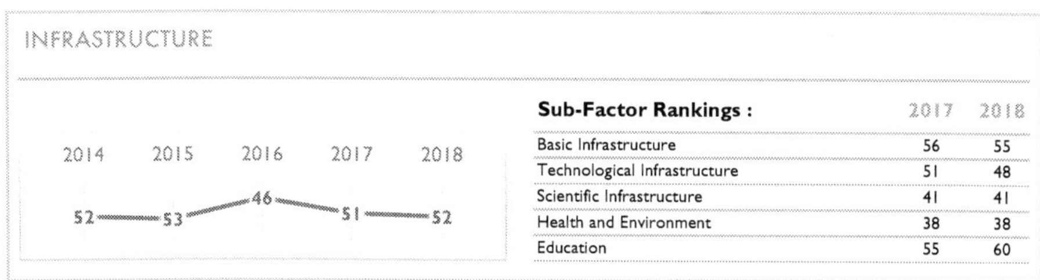

Sub-Factor Rankings :	2017	2018
Basic Infrastructure	56	55
Technological Infrastructure	51	48
Scientific Infrastructure	41	41
Health and Environment	38	38
Education	55	60

Source: IMD World Competitiveness Yearbook 2018

and the health and environment sub-category remained the same as well, ranking at 38. Education fell from 55 down to 60.

A CLOSER LOOK AT VENEZUELA

Venezuela has the least competitive economy in the world. Why is it failing? Each of the four factors have an overall score of 63, and every category falls on the opposite side of the ranking system from the best economies. Let's examine the factors and subfactors:

The economic performance factor has an overall score of 63 and has remained stagnant from 2017. Four of the five sub-factors in this factor have remained the same as the year before. Domestic economy, international trade, and prices have remained at 63. International investment has remained at 60. Employment has gotten worse from 59 to 60.

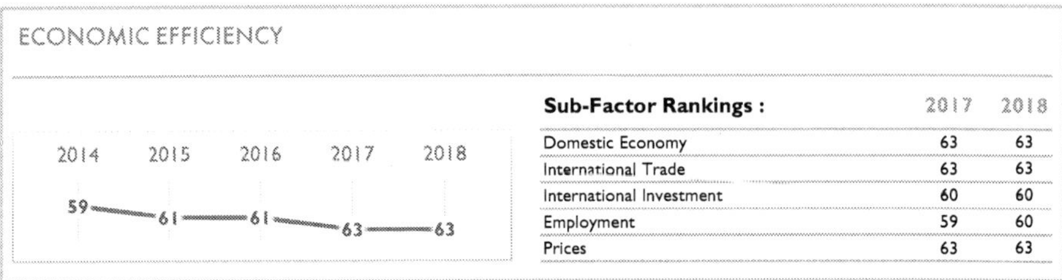

Sub-Factor Rankings :	2017	2018
Domestic Economy	63	63
International Trade	63	63
International Investment	60	60
Employment	59	60
Prices	63	63

Source: IMD World Competitiveness Yearbook 2018

The government efficiency factor also has an overall score of 63 and hasn't improved in a years. The sub-factors public finance has gotten much worse since 2017, dropping from 42 to 62 while the tax policy improved from 13 to 8. The other three categories institutional framework, business legislation, and societal framework have all remained at 63 for the past two years.

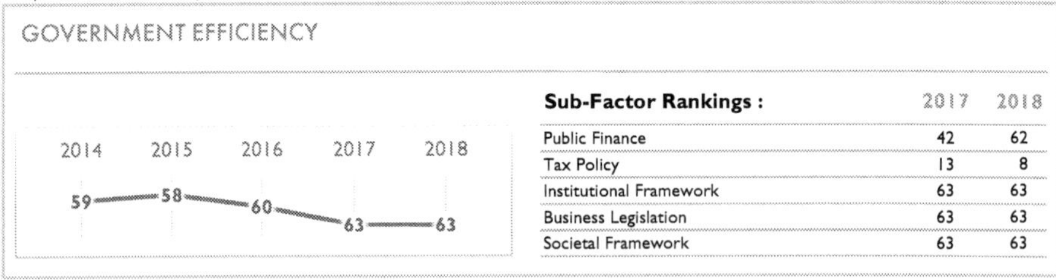

Sub-Factor Rankings :	2017	2018
Public Finance	42	62
Tax Policy	13	8
Institutional Framework	63	63
Business Legislation	63	63
Societal Framework	63	63

Source: IMD World Competitiveness Yearbook 2018

The business efficiency factor's overall score worsened from 61 to 63. The sub-factor productivity & efficiency dropped from 62 to 63, while the labour market

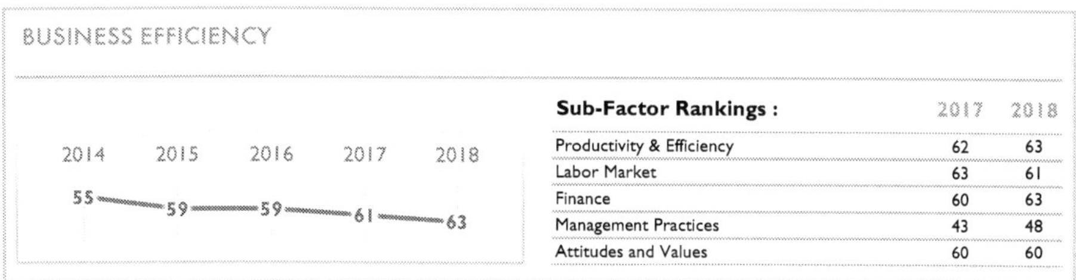

Sub-Factor Rankings :	2017	2018
Productivity & Efficiency	62	63
Labor Market	63	61
Finance	60	63
Management Practices	43	48
Attitudes and Values	60	60

Source: IMD World Competitiveness Yearbook 2018

improved a bit from 63 to 61. Finance worsened from 60 to 63, and management practices dropped in ranking from 43 to 48. The attitude and value stayed the same at 60.

Infrastructure has remained stagnant at 63 for the past two years. Basic infrastructure and technological structure have both remained stagnant at a ranking of 63 for

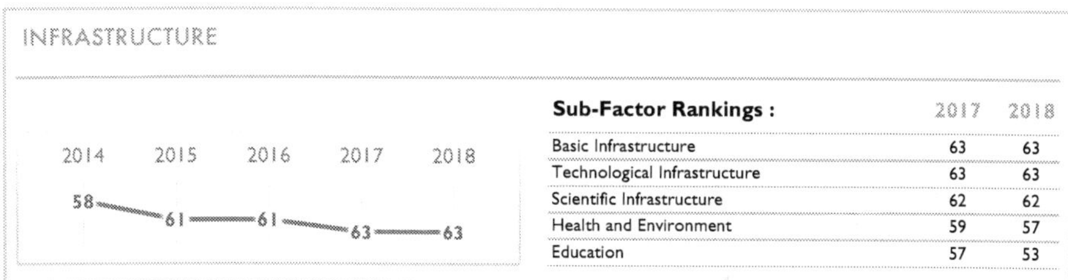

Sub-Factor Rankings :	2017	2018
Basic Infrastructure	63	63
Technological Infrastructure	63	63
Scientific Infrastructure	62	62
Health and Environment	59	57
Education	57	53

Source: IMD World Competitiveness Yearbook 2018

two years. Scientific structure has remained at a ranking of 62, while health and environment has improved from 59 to 57. Education has improved slightly from 57 to 53.

SUMMARY

The economies that possess the best potential for offering a better quality of life appear to do well in at least two of the four main factors, although no two countries take the same approach. For example, the U S does well in the areas of infrastructure and economic performance, which can be attributed to the entrepreneurial culture and political system. However, U.S. President Donald J. Trump has cut corporate regulations and changed trade agreements and tariffs, which has in the short term improved the overall competitiveness of America's economy.

Hong-Kong has had a uniquely different political system and social culture, this creates an environment conducive to economic growth and competitiveness. Hong-Kong does well in with government efficiency and business efficiency, but lags behind the U.S. in other areas.

Although each country takes a different path towards competitiveness, there is undoubtedly a large disparity connected to their body of government, culture, and openness.

Venezuela's political instability has harmed its competitiveness forcing it to remain stagnant and worsened over time. The people of Venezuela suffer because they cannot obtain a better quality of life which may ultimately lead to violence, according to Ted Gurr's Relative Deprivation Theory[1]. The relative deprivation theory states that when people try to do what it takes to obtain a better quality of life, but never experience a shift upward on the socio-economic spectrum, they will resort to violence.

FOOTNOTES

Chapter 1

1. Coase R., 'The Nature of the Firm', Economica, 1937
2. 'The retreat of the global company', The Economist, 28 Jan 2017
3. Schechner S., 'Facebook faces potential 1.63 billion fine in Europe over data breach', Wall Street Journal, 30 Sept 2017
4. Jefferson T., 'Thomas Jefferson to George Logan', 12 Nov 1816, available via: Princeton University Press, https://founders.archives.gov/documents/Jefferson/03-10-02-0390
5. Manyika J., Lund S., Bughin J. et al., 'Independent work: choice, necessity and the gig-economy', McKinsey Global Institute, Oct 2016

Chapter 2

1. Weber M., 'The theory of social and economic organisation' (New York, Oxford University Press, 1947)
2. McCarthy E. J., 1979, via: https://www.goodreads.com/quotes/7287536

Chapter 3

1. Rauch, Ori Brafman and Rod A. Beckstrom The Starfish and the Spider, 2006
2. 'Toyota Production System', Wikipedia, 28 Nov 2018, via: https://en.wikipedia.org/wiki/Toyota_Production_System
3. Beck K., Beedle M., Van Bennekom A., et al., 'Manifesto for agile software development', Agile Manifesto, 2001, http://agilemanifesto.org/
4. ING Belgium, 'Agile way of working in ING Belgium', [Video file], Youtube, 29 Sept 2017, retrieved from: https://www.youtube.com/watch?v=TaV-d7eKWFc
5. Cornish L., '6 organisations to watch among NGO Advisor's top-ranked 500', Devex, 6 Feb 2017
6. Rigby D., Sutherland J. and Noble A., 'Agile at Scale', Harvard Business Review, May 2018

7. 'Netflix culture', Netflix, https://jobs.netflix.com/culture
8. Woudt J., 'Helemaal geen kantoor is voor Microsoft toch the wild', Financieel Dagblad, 1 Nov 2018

Chapter 4

1. Cohn, D. and Caumont A., '10 demographic trends that are shaping the U.S. and the world', Pew Research Center, 31 March 2016
2. Basso H., 'How will an ageing economy affect the economy?', World Economic Forum, 9 Apr 2015

Chapter 5

1. Beall G., '8 key differences between Gen Z and millenials', Huffington Post, 6 Nov 2017
2. Welzel, C., 'Freedom Rising: Human Empowerment and the Quest for Emancipation' New York: Cambridge University Press, 2013
3. Pinker S., Enlightenment Now: The Case for Reason, Science, Humanism, and Progress. (Viking, 2018)
4. Piketty T., Capital in the Twenty-First century, (Harvard University Press, 2014)
5. Becchetti L., Castriota S. and Depedri S., 'Working in the for-profit versus not-for-profit sector: what difference does it make? An inquiry on preferences of voluntary and involuntary movers', Industrial and Corporate Change, 23(4), 1 Aug 2014
6. 'PwC Young Workers Index', PWC UK, Oct 2017
7. 'How an ageing workforce can revitalise your business', ACAS, 2017, available from: http://www.acas.org.uk/index.aspx?articleid=5919
8. 'The future of jobs', World Economic Forum, Jan 2016

Chapter 6

1. Willits D. The Pinch: How the Baby Boomers Took Their Children's Future – And Why They Should Give It Back, (Atlantic Books, 2010)
2. 'Megatrends: Demographic and Social Changes', PWC, 2018, available

from: https://www.pwc.co.uk/issues/megatrends/demographic-and-social-change.html

3. 'A Major Survey Targeting the US, Brazil, Singapore and Switzerland', Credit Suisse Group AG, 2017
4. Dellot B. and Wallace-Stephens F., 'Good work in the age of radical technology', The RSA, 24 Sept 2017
5. Phillips D., Curtice J., Phillips M. and Perry J., British Social Attitudes: The 35th Report (London: The National Centre for Social Research, 2018)
6. PwC,'Workforce of the Future: The competing forces shaping 2030', PwC, 2018
7. Dellot B. and Wallace-Stephens S., 'Good work in an age of radical technologies', The RSA, 24 Sept 2018
8. TUC, 'I'll be watching you', TUC, 17 Aug 2018
9. See Glossary of Terms
10. Hunt V., Yee L., Prince S. and Dixon-Fyle S. 'Delivering through diversity', McKinsey, Jan 2018

Chapter 7

1. Schwab K. and Zahidi S., '10 things you - and your government - should know about competitiveness in the Fourth Industrial Revolution', World Economic Forum, 18 Oct 2018
2. Amadeo K., 'What is competitive advantage? Three strategies that work', The Balance, 29 Oct 2018
3. Gurr T. R., Handbook of political conflict: theory and research, (New York, Free Press, 1980)
4. Hogan D., 'Why is Singapore's school system so successful, and is it a model for the West?' The Conversation, 11 Feb 2014
5. Kent D.C., 'A new educational perspective: The case of Singapore', Penn GSE Perspectives on Urban Education, Fall 2017, Vol(14);1
6. Erickson A., 'What's behind the student suicides sweeping Hong Kong?', The Washington Post, 25 Feb 2017

7. Chan W., 'A Review of Educational Reform – New Senior Secondary (NSS) Education in Hong Kong', International Education Studies, Nov 2010, Vol.3(4), p.26-35
8. Cheung M., 'Hong Kong: Government Investing in Education', 7th Space, 18 Jan 2019
9. '2018 Index of Economic Freedom: Hong Kong', The Heritage Foundation, 2018, p.214-215, available from: https://www.heritage.org/index/country/hongkong
10. '2018 Index of Economic Freedom: Singapore', The Heritage Foundation, 2018, p.368-369, available from: https://www.heritage.org/index/country/singapore
11. Bajpai P., 'Hong Kong versus China: Understand the differences', Investopedia, 21 March 2018
12. Chen J., 'Government Of Singapore Investment Corporation - GIC', Investopedia, 31 May 2018
13. Bender M. C., Rubin R. & Timiraos N., 'Trump Wants Tax Plan to Cut Corporate Rate to 15%' The Wall Street Journal, 24 Apr 2017
14. '2018 Index of Economic Freedom: United States', The Heritage Foundation, 2018, p.426-427, available from: https://www.heritage.org/index/country/unitedstates

Chapter 8

1. Bowles J., 'Chart of the Week: 54% of EU jobs at risk of computerisation', Bruegel, 24 July 2014
2. Frey C.B. and Osborne M.A., 'The future of employment: how susceptible are jobs to computerisation?', Technological Forecasting & Social Change, Jan 2017, Vol.114, p.254-280
3. 'Job automation risks vary widely across different regions within countries', OECD, 18 Sept 2018
4. OECD, Job Creation and Local Economic Development 2018: Preparing for the Future of Work (Paris, OECD Publishing, 2018)

5. Cooper Y., 'Automation could destroy millions of jobs. We have to deal with it now', The Guardian, 6 Aug 2018
6. Forum Human Rights et al., 'Civil society threatened all over the world', Dec 2016
7. Levy F. and Murnane R.J., The new division of labour: How computers are creating the next job market, (Princeton University Press, 2005)
8. Jee C., 'Google's AI is better at spotting advanced breast cancer than pathologists', The Download, 15 Oct 2018
9. Hamer A., 'Moravec's Paradox Is Why the Easy Stuff Is Hardest for Artificial Intelligence', Curiosity, 11 June 2018
10. McKinsey Global Institute, 'Jobs lost, jobs gained: workforce transition in a time of automation', McKinsey & Company, Dec 2017

Chapter 9

1. Forrest C., 'Chinese factory replaces 90 percent of human workers with robots, production soars', TechRepublic, 30 July 2015
2. Culey S., 'Revitalizing the Rust Belt', Forbes, 8 Sept 2017
3. Sawhill I., The Forgotten Americans: An Economic Agenda for a Divided Nation, (Yale University Press, Sept 2018)
4. Saez E. and Piketty T., 'Striking it Richer: The Evolution of Top Incomes in the United States', UC Berkeley, 30 June 2016
5. Keeley B., 'Income Inequality: The Gap between Rich and Poor', OECD Insights, Dec 2015
6. Mudde C., 'How populism became the concept that defines our age', The Guardian, 22 Nov 2018
7. Walters J., 'Americans show support for Obamacare despite Trump's repeal attempts', The Guardian, 9 Nov 2017
8. Naim M. and Toro F., 'Venezuela's suicide', Foreign Affairs, Nov/Dec 2018
9. 'Switzerland Minimum Wage', Minimum Wage, available from: https://www.minimum-wage.org/international/switzerland
10. EurWork, 'Finland: wage information', Eurofound, 30 Mar 2009

Chapter 10

1. 'The size of the global sharing economy', PwC, 2017
2. 'Key Figures', Etsy investor relations, available from: https://investors.etsy.com/overview/key-figures/default.aspx
3. Adkins A., 'Millennials: the job-hopping generation', Workplace, 12 May 2016, Gallup
4. Bartleby, 'The high costs of staff turnover', The Economist, 22 Sept 2018
5. Campbell A. F., 'New York City passes nation's first minimum pay rate for Uber and Lyft drivers', Vox, 5 Dec 2018
6. 'Worries about the rise of the gig economy are mostly overblown', The Economist, 4 Oct 2018
7. 'New York votes to cap Uber and Lyft services', BBC News, 9 Aug 2018

Chapter 11

1. Manyika J., Chui M., Miremadi M. et al., 'A future that works: Automation, Employment and Productivity', McKinsey Global Institute, January 2017.
2. 'The impact of automation on jobs', PwC, 2018, available from: https://www.pwc.co.uk/services/economics-policy/insights/the-impact-of-automation-on-jobs.html
3. Allen T., 'Bank of England sounds warning note over automation job losses', V3 UK, 20 Aug 2018
4. Turner A. 'The high-tech, high-touch economy', Project Syndicate, 16 Apr 2016
5. See Glossary of Terms
6. Wakabayashi D., Griffith E., Tsang A. and Conger K., 'Google Walkout: Employees Stage Protest Over Handling of Sexual Harassment',The New York Times, 1 Nov 2018
7. For an overview of statistics by OECD, see: https://stats.oecd.org
8. Butler S., 'Deliveroo couriers win six-figure payout in employment rights case', The Guardian, 28 June 2018

Chapter 12

1. Central Bureau of Statistics, 'Flexwerk in Nederland en de EU', 2017, available from: https://www.cbs.nl/nl-nl/dossier/dossier-flexwerk/hoofdcategorieen/flexwerk-in-nederland-en-de-eu
2. Manyika J., Lund S., Bughin J. et al., 'Independent work: choice, necessity and the gig-economy', McKinsey Global Institute, Oct 2016
3. 'Netherlands unemployment rate', Trading Economics, available from: https://tradingeconomics.com/netherlands/unemployment-rate
4. Blom M., 'Platformen kunnen arbeidsmarkt drastisch veranderen', ING Economisch Bureau, 28 Nov 2018

Chapter 13

1. Ogilvie S., 'The Economics of Guilds', Journal of Economic Perspectives, 2014, Vol. 28(4)
2. Mobius M. M. and Schoenle R., 'The evolution of work', National Bureau of Economic Research, Jan 2006
3. Stanley M., 'The Gig economy goes global', Morgan Stanley, 4 June 2018
4. 'If companies had no employees', The Economist; 12 July 2018
5. Huizinga R., Bris A., Blockchange!, (Amsterdam, TROI Studio BV, 2018)

Chapter 14

1. McKinsey Global Institute, 'Jobs lost, jobs gained: workforce transition in a time of automation', McKinsey & Company, Dec 2017
2. Gaille B., '29 interesting entrepreneur demographics', Brandon Gaille, 31 Dec 2015
3. The Economist Intelligence Unit, 'Informal Innovation', The Economist, 2016, available from: http://informalinnovation.economist.com/
4. U.S. Department of health, education and welfare, Technology and the American economy, Feb 1966, Chapter 2, p. 9
5. Michel A., 'This is the education reform America needs', Huffington Post, 2 Oct 2017

Chapter 15

1. Backman M., 'What the average American has -and needs- in emergency savings', The Motley Fool, 21 May 2018
2. 'How many income streams should you have?' Passive Income MD, Nov 2018
3. Bloom E., 'Here's how many Americans are living paycheck to paycheck', CNBC Makit, 29 June 2017
4. Webb M. S., 'Life begins at 60 – with consequences for all of us', Financial Times, 9 Nov 2018
5. Manyika J., Lund S., Bughin J. et al., 'Independent work: choice, necessity and the gig-economy', McKinsey Global Institute, Oct 2016
6. Farrington R., 'The most common multiple income streams', The College Investor, Jan 2019

Chapter 17

1. Delle Fave A., Brdar I., Wissing M.P. et al. 'Lay Definitions of Happiness across Nations: The Primacy of Inner Harmony and Relational Connectedness', Front Psychol, 26 Jan 2016, Vol.7(30)
2. Pinker S., Enlightenment Now: The Case for Reason, Science, Humanism, and Progress. (Viking, 2018)
3. Our world in data, 'GDP per capita versus self-reported life satisfaction', Our World in Data, 2016, available from: https://ourworldindata.org/grapher/gdp-vs-happiness?time=2016
4. Helliwell J., Layard R. and Sachs, J. 'World Happiness Report 2018', New York: Sustainable Development Solutions Network, 2018
5. Buettner D., 'The Secrets of a Long Life', National Geographic, Nov 2005

Chapter 18

1. Jebb A. T., Tay L., Diener E. and Oishi S., 'Happiness, income satiation and turning points around the world', Nature Human Behaviour, 8 Jan 2018, Vol.2, p.33-38

2. Mr. Money Mustache, 'The 4% Rule: The Easy Answer to "How Much Do I Need for Retirement?"', Mr. Money Mustache, 29 May 2012
3. Clifton J., 'The happiest and unhappiest countries in the world', Gallup, 20 March 2017
4. Kahneman D. and Deaton A., 'High Income Improves Evaluation of Life But Not Emotional Well Being', PNAS 6 Sept 2010, Vol.107(38), p.16489-16493
5. Quoidbach J., Dunn E.W., Petrides K.V. and Mikolajczak M., 'Money giveth, money taketh away: The dual effect of wealth on happiness', Psychol Sci, Jun 2010, Vol.21(6), p.759–763.
6. Covey S.R., The 7 Habits of Highly Effective People. (Free Press, 1989)
7. Martina Huynh, Student Design Academy Basic Income Cafe 2018 http://martinahuynh.com/basic_income_cafe.html
8. Summers L., 'A jobs guarantee — progressives' latest big idea', Financial Times, 2 July 2018

Chapter 20

1. KPMG International, 'Future state 2030: Global megatrends shaping governments', Mowat Centre, Feb 2014
2. IPCC, 'Summary for Policymakers. In: Global warming of 1.5°C', World Meteorological Organization, 2018
3. 'OECD Stats', OECD, 2018, available from: https://stats.oecd.org/
4. World Bank, 'Information and Communications for Development: maximizing mobile', Aug 2012
5. McKinsey Global Institute, 'Jobs lost, jobs gained: workforce transition in a time of automation', McKinsey & Company, Dec 2017
6. Kibasi T., Jacobs M., Colebrook C. et al., 'Prosperity and justice: A plan for the new economy', IPPR, 5 Sept 2018
7. Institute for Work and Health, 'Unemployment and mental health, Institute for Work and Health, Aug 2009
8. 'Loneliness is a serious public-health problem', The Economist, 1 Sept 2018

Chapter 21

1. 'As firms struggle with seasonal hiring, Amazon turns to automation', The Economist, 24 Nov 2018
2. McKinsey Global Institute, 'Jobs lost, jobs gained: workforce transition in a time of automation', McKinsey & Company, Dec 2017
3. Dweck C., Mindset: TMindset - Updated Edition: Changing The Way You think To Fulfil Your Potential, (Robinson, 2017)
4. Leonhardt M., 'How much debt Americans have at every age', CNBC, 20 Aug 2018
5. Huddleston C., 'Americans are drowning in debts', GoBankingRates, 8 Nov 2018
6. Shonkoff J.P. and Phillips D.A., From Neurons to Neighbourhoods: The Science of Early Childhood Development. (National Research Council (US) and Institute of Medicine (US) Committee on Integrating the Science of Early Childhood Development, 2000)
7. Bughin J., Lund S. and Hazan E., 'Automation will make life long learning a necessary part of work', Harvard Business Review, 24 May 2018
8. The World Bank, 'World Bank Development report 2016', Digital Dividend, 17 May 2016
9. Handy C., 'Educating for uncertainty', London Business School Review, 3 Dec 2018, Vol.29(3); p.10-11
10. Cobb J., 12 Trends (Still) Disrupting the Market for Lifelong Learning and Continuing Education', Leading Learning, 20 March 2018
11. Ducard M., 'What brands can learn from educational content on YouTube', Think with Google, May 2017
12. Glaeser E., Triumph of the City: How Our Greatest Invention Makes Us Richer, Smarter, Greener, Healthier, and Happier, (Pan MacMillan, 2011)

Appendix A

1. Gurr T. R., Handbook of political conflict: theory and research, (New York, Free Press, 1980)

FLEX OR FAIL - ARTURO BRIS, TONY FELTON & ROBBY MOL

Printed in Great Britain
by Amazon